Play in Renais

'Let's joke, but seriously' (*scherzare, sì, ma seriamente*)
In memory of Umberto Eco, playful scholar

Contents

Preface vi

1. Introduction 1
2. Fun and Games 21
3. Laughter 40
4. Play: For and Against 74
5. Who, Where and When? 87
6. New Trends 123
7. Epilogue: Beyond 1650 138

Dramatis Personae 147
Further Reading 155
Index 159

Preface

A Chinese painter, explaining to his pupils how to paint a grove of bamboo, told them to meditate for months on bamboo, to try to become a bamboo, and then produce their painting in a matter of minutes. In similar fashion, this essay in synthesis, although short and written in the course of a few months, has been long in the making. Writing about festivals, and in particular about Carnival, in my *Popular Culture in Early Modern Europe* (1978) made me want to continue in this direction. Conversations with Philippe Ariès a few months later led to an invitation to give a paper at a conference in Tours in 1980 concerned with 'Les jeux à la Renaissance'. A conference on 'tempo libero', held in Prato in 1992, allowed me to explore the history of the idea of leisure. Writing a book about Castiglione's *Courtier*, a dialogue that is presented as a game, encouraged thought about playfulness in the culture of the High Renaissance. A conference on the cultural history of humour, organized by Jan Bremmer and Herman Roodenburg and held in Amsterdam, was the occasion

Preface

for a paper on 'Frontiers of the Comic', that turned into a chapter in a collective study of the history of humour, published in 1997.[1] In short, I feel that I have been preparing for this essay for more than forty years without knowing it. I have occasionally stolen sentences from my past self in order to construct it, but I believe that this book offers new ideas as well as developing thoughts that were originally expressed in print elsewhere in new directions.

Another invitation, this time from John Henderson and Virginia Cox, to write a short book for a series of studies of the Italian Renaissance, persuaded me to return to the subject. I do not wish to thank the recent virus, but its result, virtual confinement at home, concentrated the mind wonderfully and allowed me to put my notes in order and produce a first draft while major libraries were closed. I cannot thank my wife Maria Lúcia enough for looking after me in that time of crisis. Telling stories was a form of light relief for the group of young men and women described in Boccaccio's *Decameron* – refugees from the plague of 1348 – and doubtless for the author himself. For me in 2020, reading and writing about play was a form of light relief from a world dominated by the Coronavirus.

---

[1] Peter Burke, *Popular Culture in Early Modern Europe* (1978; 3rd edn, Farnham, 2009); 'Le carnaval de Venise', in Philippe Ariès and Jean-Claude Margolin (eds.) *Les jeux à la Renaissance* (Paris, 1982), 55–64; Burke, *The Fortunes of the Courtier* (Cambridge, 1995); Burke, 'The Invention of Leisure in Early Modern Europe', *Past and Present* 146 (1995), 136–50; Burke, 'Frontiers of the Comic in Early Modern Italy', in Jan Bremmer and Herman Roodenburg (eds.) *A Cultural History of Humour* (Cambridge, 1997), 61–75.

1
Introduction

The three principal words in the title of this book may seem clear, but each of them is problematic. 'Italy' in this period might be said to be both too small and too large a unit of study. On one side, traditional forms of play in Italy, from charivaris (*scampanate*) to Carnival, had parallels elsewhere in Europe, while some new forms invented in Italy, such as the comedy, were adopted and adapted in other countries. On the other side, Italy was not yet a nation but a number of regions, which varied in their cultures as well as in their economies and political systems. A written language based on Tuscan was helping to unify the peninsula at this time, but the majority of the population spoke regional dialects, and the elites often employed dialect as a playful form of language, as we shall see.

Readers will notice that the majority of the examples offered in the book come from northern and central Italy. This does not mean that play stopped south of Rome. Obvious examples to the contrary include the storyteller Masuccio Salernitano, from Salerno in southwest

Italy; Pietro Antonio Caracciolo, an actor who wrote farces in his native Neapolitan; Fabrizio de Fornaris, another Neapolitan actor who was famous for his rendering of the boastful but cowardly 'Captain Crocodile'; Giambattista della Porta, a polymath from Naples who is best known for his comedies; and Giordano Bruno, from Nola near Naples, the author of some lively and playful dialogues. The minor role played by the south in this essay is probably the result of a relative lack of evidence. The Sicilian puppet theatre, for instance, already existed at this time, but little is known about the performances before the nineteenth century.

The term 'Renaissance' is also problematic. The main problem is the contrast between two common usages. The term is often employed in the traditional manner to describe a period of European history – more or less, the fifteenth and sixteenth centuries. Nowadays, this period is more often described as 'early modern' and extended to the eighteenth century. In this essay, I shall be looking at Italy during a long Renaissance from 1350 to 1650.

The word 'Renaissance' is also used in a more precise and limited sense to refer to a movement, a collective attempt to recover and imitate the culture of classical antiquity (Greek and Roman). The focus of this essay will be on the movement, extended to include the work of the major artists and writers of the period, even when they were not inspired by the ancient world. The movement involved only a minority of the Italian population, but to place it in context it will be necessary to examine popular culture as well.

Do we have too serious a view of the Renaissance? It certainly had a playful side, and so did many – if not the majority – of the most famous individuals who con-

Introduction

tributed to the movement, whether they were artists or scholars (the so-called 'humanists').

Leading artists, including Leonardo (whose notebooks show that he also collected jokes), Raphael (whose playful cherubs have become iconic), Bronzino (whose comic poems show he was not as cold as his paintings may suggest), Giulio Romano (who made architectural jokes) and Arcimboldo (who invented visual puns), all produced images that were intended to provoke a laugh, or at least a smile. Even Michelangelo, often regarded as completely serious – either in agony or in ecstasy – had a sense of humour that was expressed in his poems (mocking himself at work on the Sistine ceiling) as well as in his art, and, according to legend, in practical jokes as well. He exchanged comic verses with the master of that genre at the time, Francesco Berni.[1]

Leading humanists, including Petrarch, Poggio Bracciolini, Angelo Poliziano and Pietro Bembo, collected jests. Cosimo de' Medici, the unofficial ruler of Florence, plays an active role in Poliziano's jestbook. Cosimo's grandson Lorenzo de' Medici wrote songs for Carnival as well as a comic poem, and Lorenzo's second son, Giovanni – who became Pope Leo X – employed several fools to entertain himself and his court. Baldassare Castiglione discussed the nature of

---

[1] On Bronzino, Deborah Parker, 'Toward a Reading of Bronzino's Burlesque Poetry', *Renaissance Quarterly* 50 (1997), 1011–44; on Giulio Romano, Paul Barolsky, *Infinite Jest: Wit and Humor in Italian Renaissance Art* (Columbia, MO, 1978), 75–100, 132–8; on Arcimboldo, Thomas DaCosta Kaufmann, *Arcimboldo: Visual Jokes, Natural History and Still-Life Painting* (Chicago, IL, 2010); on Michelangelo, Barolsky, *Infinite Jest*, 51–74, and Antonio Corsaro, 'Michelangelo, il comico e la malinconia', in *La regola e la licenza: studi sulla poesia satirica e burlesca fra cinque e seicento* (Rome, 1999), 115–33.

Play in Renaissance Italy

humour. Niccolò Machiavelli wrote comedies. Great ladies, notably Isabella d'Este, took part in games. The humanist Leonbattista Alberti presented mathematical puzzles as 'jolly things' (*cose jocundissime*). Philosophers from Marsilio Ficino to Giordano Bruno were attracted by the idea of 'serious play' (*serio ludere* or *giocare serio*), while Galileo included comic passages in his lively dialogue 'Concerning the Two Main World Systems' (1632).[2] Among the greatest Italian poets of the period, Ludovico Ariosto wrote comedies and a playful romance, *Orlando furioso*, while Torquato Tasso wrote dialogues about games.

Insofar as the Renaissance was a movement of cultural innovation – sometimes disguised as renovation – some observations by psychologists may be illuminating. It has been suggested that innovation is encouraged by playing with ideas, trying out alternative solutions to a given problem. Dialogue is one form of this play, and printed dialogues, as well as oral ones, flourished in Italy at this time.[3]

Writing about play in the Renaissance is not meant to imply that there was an absence of playfulness in the Middle Ages. On the contrary, play was a powerful presence at that time, obvious enough to anyone who reads about Francis of Assisi, for example, or looks at the margins of many medieval manuscripts, or at the gargoyles or the misericords in Gothic churches.[4] There

---

[2] Ian Petru Culianu, *Iocari serio: scienza e arte nel pensiero del Rinascimento* (2003: Italian translation, Turin, 2017); Paula Findlen's 'Galileo's Laughter: Knowledge and Play in the Renaissance' remains unpublished.
[3] Weston La Barre, *Shadow of Childhood* (Norman, OK, 1991), 109; Virginia Cox, *The Renaissance Dialogue* (Cambridge, 1992).
[4] Jacques Le Goff, 'Le rire médiéval entre la cour et la place publique', in

Introduction

were important continuities in forms of play between the Middle Ages and Renaissance, notably in the case of Carnival, as well as forms that broke with tradition.

What is Play?

The third problem is the most complex and difficult of all. What is play? What has a fist-fight to do with a guessing game, a comedy or a parody? Among the many theorists of play who have wrestled with this question, I should like to single out three: a Dutchman, a Frenchman and a Russian.[5]

In his essay *Homo Ludens* (1938), probably the best-known study of the subject, the Dutch historian Johan Huizinga examined what he called 'the play element in culture', ranging from war to the pursuit of knowledge. What did Huizinga mean by play? He suggested that it is an activity undertaken for its own sake, in its own times and places; that it creates order by means of its rules; and that it is marked both by tension and its relief. He also distinguished two main forms of play: mimicry and competition.[6] In *Man, Play and Games* (1958), the French philosopher and sociologist Roger Caillois divided play into four types, adding chance and vertigo to Huizinga's pair of models. Neither scholar

---

Pauvres et riches (Warsaw, 1992), 307–11; Le Goff, 'Une enquête sur le rire', *Annales: Histoire, Sciences Sociales* 52 (1997), 449–55; Paul Hardwick (ed.) *The Playful Middle Ages* (Turnhout, 2010).

[5] On the possible contribution of theorists to the study of early modern play, Bret Rothstein, 'Early Modern Play: Three Perspectives', *Renaissance Quarterly* 71 (2018), 1036–46. The perspectives are those of Johan Huizinga, Bernard Suits and Eugen Fink.

[6] Johan Huizinga, *Homo Ludens: A Study of the Play Element in Culture* (1938: English translation, London, 1970), 26–30.

discussed either puzzles or humour.[7] The second of these gaps was filled by the Russian literary theorist Mikhail Bakhtin, whose *Problems of Dostoyevsky's Poetics* (1929) revived the ancient Greek and Roman idea of the 'serio-comic' and discussed what he called the history of laughter. Bakhtin emphasized the cultural importance of 'the carnival sense of the world' and especially the central, subversive act of Carnival, the 'mock crowning and subsequent uncrowning of the carnival king'.[8]

What follows makes use of the work of all three theorists, but, unlike them, it is concerned not with universal principles of play but with its forms and roles in a specific culture in a specific period. Many games are international – more exactly, they have been internationalized. In contrast, fun or humour, like some wines, does not travel well. What is considered playful in a given culture or a given historical period may not be found amusing in another.

To avoid this problem, one might define play as a bundle or, better, a system of practices that are recognized as playful in a particular culture. The practices resemble one another like members of a family, who share various traits though any one of these traits may be lacking in a particular individual. It may be easier to recognize what counts as play by thinking about what is excluded (the process of exclusion is discussed in Chapter 6). In Renaissance Italy, playful practices were distinguished from serious ones, and play was often jus-

---

[7] Roger Caillois, *Man, Play and Games* (1958: English translation, London, 1962).
[8] Mikhail Bakhtin, *Problems of Dostoyevsky's Poetics* (1929: English translation, Manchester, 1984), 106–9, 32–6, 124, 131.

Introduction

What these terms have in common is their opposition to *noia*, at that time a word with a range of meanings for unpleasant feelings such as sadness and anxiety. To poets, the contrast and the rhyme of *gioia* and *noia* proved irresistible. *Annoiare* meant 'to bother someone', while *noisoso* meant 'fussy'. In Renaissance Ferrara, the ruler built a villa near the city and named it Schifanoia, 'avoid *noia*'. Although life was absurdly short, as Renaissance poets regularly remarked, time often hung heavily on people's hands, to judge by the popularity of terms such as *passatempo* or *fuggilozio* ('avoid idleness' – or, perhaps, 'find something to do'). The idea of boredom is said to have emerged only in the eighteenth century, but it is surely hiding behind some of the terms listed above, together with 'tedious' (*tedioso*).[12]

Other terms were more precise. *Inganno* meant 'deceit', itself a keyword that will recur in this essay, just as the practice recurred in Italy at this time. *Burla* was defined by Castiglione in his famous *Book of the Courtier* (*Il Cortegiano*) as 'a friendly trick' (*un inganno amichevole*). The literary term 'burlesque' is derived from it, and a leading comic poet of the sixteenth century, Francesco Berni, was described by a colleague as 'master and father of the burlesque style' (*maestro e padre del burlesco stile*). *Beffa* refers to a practical joke, a common practice in Renaissance Italy – a word that generated related terms such as the adjectives *beffardo* and *beffabile*. The term *scherzo* ranged from child's play to adult wit.

---

[12] Patricia M. Spacks, *Boredom: The Literary History of a State of Mind* (Chicago, IL, 1995). Scipione Bargagli wrote about Carnival games filling 'tedious nights' (quoted in Laura Riccò, *Giuoco e teatro nelle veglie di Siena* (Rome, 1993), 118.

Play in Renaissance Italy

An important cluster of words centred on the idea of madness (*pazzia*) and included 'oddities' (*bizarrie*), 'caprices' (*capricci*), 'whims' (*ghiribizzi*) and 'eccentricities' (*stravaganze*), all terms that may now seem negative but were used at the time in a positive manner as well. They were associated with jesters and clowns (*buffoni*), some of them much admired at court as well as in the piazza, and also with creative individuals such as Leonardo, whose *ghiribizzi* are described in the life of the artist by Giorgio Vasari. These terms were also employed on the title-pages of comic texts as a kind of advertisement. Take the case of the Venetian comic actor Andrea Calmo, whose letters were published under the title *Cherebizzi* (a dialect form of *ghiribizzi*), while his verses were described as concerned with 'ridiculous and bizarre subjects' (*soggetti ridicolosi e bizzarri*). Calmo's contemporary Alessandro Caravia, a goldsmith and a comic poet, recounted the exploits of a sympathetic ruffian under the title *Naspo Bizzarro* (1565).

In the Middle Ages, only a few of these terms were in use, among them *buffone, derisione, diletto, diporto, giocare, ludere, recreazione, solazzo, spasso, svagare* ('to amuse') and *trastullo* ('pleasure'). A witty saying was already described as a *motto*, while to produce one was known as *motteggiare*. In the fourteenth century, the writer Giovanni Boccaccio used the words *beffa, festevole* ('light-hearted'), *piacevole* (which meant 'witty' as well as 'courteous'), *scherzare, trastullare* ('to deceive') and *trattenimento*, ('entertainment').

If texts are to be trusted (since they usually lag behind speech), the number of words available to describe forms of play expanded in the fifteenth and sixteenth centuries. In the fifteenth century, we find *baia*, a synonym

Introduction

for *beffa*; *canzonare* ('to joke'); *ciurmare* ('to deceive'); *furbo* ('trickster') – a term still common in Italy, with a positive meaning; *ludicro* ('funny'); *mottevole* ('witty'); *scherzo* ('joke'); *stravagante* ('over the top'); and *uccellare* ('to fool').

In the sixteenth century, leading Renaissance writers such as Aretino, Ariosto, Bembo, Berni, Castiglione, Grazzini, Machiavelli and Vasari added terms such as *acutezza* ('wit'); *arguzia* ('shrewdness' or 'wit'); *bagatelle* ('frivolities'); *bizzaro*; *buffoneria*; *burla, burlesco*; *capriccio, capriccioso*; *commedia* (in the sense of 'comedy'); *faceto* ('witty'); *furbesco* ('sly'); *ghiribizzi*; *giocamente* ('for fun'); *grottesco* ('grotesque'); *passatempo*; *pazzeggiare* ('to act like a mad person'); *piacevolezze*; *ridicolo* and *ridicoloso*. The proliferation of words is surely a sign that more attention is being given to play than before, a conclusion that is confirmed by the rising number of treatises on particular games, and the learned discussion of the nature of humour.

In what follows, Chapter 2 describes forms of play in Renaissance Italy. Italians of the period played many games, including mock-battles and the ancestors of football, tennis, and some 'parlour games'. Chapter 3 is concerned with different kinds of humour, in words, images and actions, from comedies to practical jokes. Chapter 4 discusses the debate about play, the critics and the defenders. Chapter 5 adopts a sociological approach, asking who played, where and when. Chapter 6 discusses changes over the long term, from the fourteenth to the early seventeenth century, while the Epilogue continues the discussion up to our own time. Throughout the book, I shall be concerned with the uses and functions of play, which are surely just as important as work in the construction, expression and maintenance of both individual and collective identities.

As the Further Reading makes abundantly clear, this book is very far from the first contribution to the subject. Academic historians only began to take play seriously in the last few decades, from the 1970s or 1980s onwards, but they had a long chain of predecessors, a varied, unexpected and sometimes eccentric group of pioneers.

The History of the History of Play

A concern with the history of play goes back to the Renaissance itself. Books about play, such as the treatise on games of chance by the polymath Girolamo Cardano or the dialogue on games by the Sienese patrician Girolamo Bargagli, illustrated the antiquity of games with examples from ancient Rome, while the humanist physician Girolamo Mercuriale wrote a treatise on ancient Greek and Roman gymnastics.[13] In the seventeenth century, a study of the comic poetry of the ancients was published by the poet and scholar Nicola Villani.[14] After Villani, the history of play fell out of favour. A few eighteenth-century historians, notably Ludovico Muratori and Girolamo Tiraboschi, wrote on the subject, but not very much and often with

---

[13] Girolamo Cardano, *De ludo aleae* (c. 1564: English translation, *The Book on Games of Chance*, New York, 1961); Scipione Bargagli, *Dialogo dei Giuochi* (1572: ed. Patrizia Ermini, Siena, 1982); Valerio Marchetti, 'Recherches sur le "Dialogo dei Giuochi"', in Philippe Ariès and Jean-Claude Margolin (eds.) *Les jeux à la Renaissance* (Paris, 1982), 163-833. Girolamo Mercuriale, *De arte gymnastica* (Venice, 1573). Cf. Alessandro Arcangeli and Vivian Nutton (eds.) *Girolamo Mercuriale* (Florence, 2007).

[14] Niccola Villani, *Ragionamento dello Academico Aldeano sopra la poesia giocosa de' greci, de latini, e da toscani* (Venice, 1634).

Introduction

disapproval. Muratori's dissertations on Italian medieval antiquities discussed what the author called 'public games', while Tiraboschi's history of Italian literature described the 'frivolities' (*frivolezze*) of the Renaissance academies, including the 'ridiculous names' of these organizations.[15]

In the early nineteenth century, Isaac D'Israeli, an English man of letters (as well as the father of Benjamin Disraeli), wrote an essay on the Italian academies in which, following the lead of Tiraboschi, he claimed that these 'denominations of exquisite absurdity' revealed the 'national levity' of the Italians.[16] Later in the century, in a multivolume study of the Renaissance, another man of letters, John Addington Symonds, criticized what he called the 'frivolity' of the Italian comic poet Annibale Caro.[17]

The great cultural historian Jacob Burckhardt was unusual in his day in devoting ten pages to what he called 'ridicule and joking' (*Spott und Witz*) in his famous essay on the *Civilization of the Renaissance in Italy* (1860). Viewing it as a corrective to 'the modern desire for fame', part of a larger trend that he described as 'the development of the individual', Burckhardt went on to discuss the jests attributed to the priest Arlotto Mainardi and the court fool Pietro Gonnella; the practical jokes recounted in the short stories (*novelle*) of the

---

[15] Ludovico Muratori, *Antiquitates italicae medii aevi* (Milan, 1739) dissertation 29; Girolamo Tiraboschi, *Storia della letteratura italiana*, 2nd edn, vol. VII (Modena, 1791), 140.

[16] Isaac D'Israeli (1823) 'Of the ridiculous titles assumed by the Italian academies', *Curiosities of Literature*, 2nd series (1823: London, 1866 edn), 355–9.

[17] John Addington Symonds, *Renaissance in Italy*, 7 vols. (London 1875–86), vol. II, *The Revival of Learning*, 238.

period; parodies of romances of chivalry; the Renaissance theory of laughter and the satire of 'the greatest railer of modern times', Pietro Aretino. I shall return to all these themes and individuals in later chapters.[18]

For a long time, discussions of the history of play in Italy (and elsewhere) were dominated by specialists in literature (including, of course, the theatre, a field in which there has been a long tradition of studies). Tiraboschi and D'Israeli were followed in the early twentieth century by Arturo Graf, a professor of Italian literature at the University of Turin, whose essays on comic poetry will be cited on various occasions in later chapters. In contrast, the Italian philosopher-critic Benedetto Croce, writing on what he called the 'late Renaissance', declared that the phrase 'comic poetry' (*poesia giocosa*) was a contradiction because poetry is 'always serious and severe'. Croce also denounced mock-epics as signs of 'the lowering of taste'. Thomas F. Crane, an American professor of literature, took play more seriously and devoted a chapter to what he called 'Parlor Games' (translating *giochi di sala*), in a book on social customs in sixteenth-century Italy.[19]

Crane's interest in the topic was closer to that of antiquaries and folklorists than to that of his literary colleagues. Cesare Guasti, an archivist and an admirer of Muratori, published a collection of texts describing the feast of St John the Baptist in Florence. The jour-

---

[18] Jacob Burckhardt, *Civilization of the Renaissance in Italy* (1860: English translation, London, 1944), 93–103.
[19] Benedetto Croce, 'Poesia giocosa', in *Opere*, vol. XXXIX (Bari, 1941), 78–84; Thomas F. Crane, *Italian Social Customs of the Sixteenth Century* (New Haven, CT, 1920), ch. 6.

Introduction

nalist Alessandro Ademollo wrote a history of Carnival in Rome. Giuseppe Pitrè, a pioneer of Italian folklore studies, wrote on popular customs, festivals and games in Sicily. The German scholar Aby Warburg, whose concern with the Renaissance transgressed frontiers between disciplines, studied festivals at the court of the Medici in Florence. An eccentric Englishman, William Heywood, had been active as a lawyer, a journalist and even a cowboy before he retired to Siena and began writing on what he called 'the sports of Central Italy'.[20]

Outside Italy, the story of the growing interest in play is a similar one. In France, scholarly interest in Renaissance festivals was launched at a conference in 1955.[21] In 1965, two important books on Carnival were published, one in Madrid and the other in Moscow. One author, Julio Caro Baroja, was well known in Spain as an anthropologist, a historian and a folklorist. His book has a distinguished place in the long series of studies in which the author constructed a historical anthropology of Spanish culture. Caro Baroja drew on anthropological theory, notably that of Sir James Frazer, usually to criticize it for speculation and overemphasis on pagan survivals.[22]

The second author, Mikhail Bakhtin, also criticized Frazer and the folklorists but from a rather different point of view, accusing them of a lack of 'theoretical pathos' – of collecting 'curiosities' while failing to see the world of folk humour as a whole. It is difficult to

---

[20] William Heywood, *Palio and Ponte: An Account of the Sports of Central Italy from the Age of Dante to the XXth Century* (London, 1904).
[21] Jean Jacquot (ed.) *Les fêtes de la Renaissance*, 3 vols. (Paris, 1956–75).
[22] Julio Caro Baroja, *El Carnaval* (Madrid, 1965).

say whether Bakhtin's concern with play developed out of his interest in a French writer of the Renaissance, François Rabelais, or the other way round. In any case, his study *Rabelais and his World* (written before 1940 and finally permitted to be published in the USSR in 1965) is a major contribution not only to the interpretation of a masterpiece of French literature but also to the theory of play, alongside that of Huizinga (who might have been shocked by some of the ideas of his Russian colleague, had he been able to read his work).

As noted earlier, Bakhtin emphasized the importance of disorder and the use of laughter for what he calls 'uncrowning', the symbolic destruction of an enemy. In the second place, he devoted attention to what he calls 'the material bodily lower stratum'. In a book on Rabelais, this may not seem so surprising, but in the 1940s it was still unusual for a scholar to pay so much attention to what Freud (whom Bakhtin does not mention) described as anal and genital matters. In the third place, Bakhtin stressed the role of joyous or festive violence in *Gargantua and Pantagruel*. His emphasis on joy and freedom now appears to be a kind of psychological compensation for life in the USSR at a time when both joy and freedom were in short supply.[23]

In contrast to these relatively rare contributions, there was a rapid rise of histories of play from the 1980s onwards. Where earlier studies were mainly descriptive, the more recent ones often made use of theorists of play, from Huizinga to Bakhtin and the American anthropologist Clifford Geertz, whose essay on the meaning

---

[23] Mikhail Bakhtin, *Rabelais and his World* (1965: English translation, Cambridge, MA, 1968); Caro Baroja, *El Carnaval*.

Introduction

of the cock-fight in Bali, first published in 1973, rapidly became a classic.[24] As early as 1977, a Romanian scholar, Ioan Petru Culianu, was planning a book on the theory of play in the philosophical culture of the Italian Renaissance. Culianu was murdered in mysterious circumstances in 1991 before the book was completed.[25]

It is in this context of increasing interest that the historical sociologist Norbert Elias (together with his colleague Eric Dunning) put forward a theory of sport as part of the 'civilizing process', described and analysed by Elias nearly half a century earlier.[26] The theory offers a refinement and a development of the traditional view of play as a safety-valve, offering 'the liberating excitement of a struggle involving physical exertion and skill, while limiting to a minimum the chance that anyone will get seriously hurt'.[27] The authors were well aware of the paradox of presenting sport as both a form of self-control and a means of temporary escape from it in the 'quest for excitement'. Their book was a milestone in making play a respectable topic for academics to study.

In the 2020s, it has become difficult to imagine how late that respectability was in coming. In 1983, for instance, an Italian literary historian could still complain that the theme of comic poetry in the Italian Renaissance was still neglected – though her own book did much to remedy this neglect.[28] By this time, the subject of

---

[24] Clifford Geertz, 'Deep Play', in *The Interpretation of Cultures* (New York, 1973), 412–53.
[25] Horia Corneliu Cicortaş, 'Premessa' to Culianu, *Iocari serio*, 8.
[26] Norbert Elias, *The Civilizing Process* (1939: English translation, Oxford, 1978); Elias and Eric Dunning, *Quest for Excitement: Sport and Leisure in the Civilizing Process* (Oxford, 1985).
[27] Elias and Dunning, *Quest for Excitement*, 165.
[28] Silvia Longhi, *Lusus: il capitolo burlesco nel Cinquecento* (Padua, 1983),

17

play was moving from the margin of scholarly concerns towards the centre, in sociology and anthropology as well as in history. An early example of the move was a collective study of games in the Renaissance – first a conference and then a book – organized by Philippe Ariès, a French scholar who made his name with a history of childhood. In the introduction to the book, Ariès noted that topics that historians used to dismiss as 'frivolous' had become respectable, following the rise of interest in the history of forms of solidarity and sociability.[29] A few years earlier, a team of French scholars had studied literary representations of the *beffa*.[30]

Many valuable specialized studies have been published since the 1980s. The subject has 'exploded' in the sense not only of expansion but also of fragmentation, linked to the rise and the institutionalization of new fields of study such as the history of sport and the history of the dance, marked by the foundation of societies, committees, book series and journals such as the *International Journal for the History of Sport* (1984–) and *Studies in Dance History* (1988–). Economic and social historians, in Italy and elsewhere, also discovered the history of leisure, the subject of a major conference in Prato in 1992.[31] The Benetton Foundation has been subsidizing studies of games since 1987, supporting prizes, books

---

1. On comic poetry in Latin, see Ugo E. Paoli, *Il latino maccheronico* (Florence, 1959).
[29] Ariès and Margolin (eds.) *Les jeux*, introduction.
[30] André Rochon (ed.) *Formes et significations de la beffa*, 2 vols. (Paris, 1972–5).
[31] On leisure, Peter Burke, 'The Invention of Leisure in Early Modern Europe', *Past and Present* 146 (1995), 136–50.

and the journal *Ludica* (1995–).³² Social and cultural historians have joined historians of art and literature in this collective enterprise, organized by Gherardo Ortalli and others.³³

So many studies of different forms of play in Renaissance Italy have been published in the last thirty or forty years that there is not space to mention them all here. The suggestions for 'Further Reading' at the end of this book are confined to studies available in English, such as Alessandro Arcangeli on dancing, Robert Davis on the 'fist wars', Robert Henke on the *commedia dell'arte*, George McClure on parlour games, and Gherardo Ortalli on games of chance.

Many other important contributions are accessible to readers of Italian, French or German. Wordplay, satire and parody have been analysed by a team of Italian scholars, including Antonio Corsaro, Silvia Longhi and Paolo Procaccioli. In the case of Carnival, the French historian Martine Boiteux has written on Rome, and the Italian anthropologist Domenico Scafoglio on Naples. The German art historian Horst Bredekamp has studied football in Florence, and the Italian historian Alessandra Rizzi has written on Italian games in the late Middle Ages.³⁴

---

³² Barbara C. Bowen, *Humour and Humanism in the Renaissance* (Aldershot, 2004); Rochon (ed.) *Formes*. Cf. Peter Burke, 'Frontiers of the Comic in Early Modern Italy', in Jan Bremmer and Herman Roodenburg (eds.) *A Cultural History of Humour* (Cambridge, 1997), 61–75.
³³ Barolsky, *Infinite Jest*; Francesca Alberti, *La peinture facétieux* (Arles, 2016).
³⁴ Antonio Corsaro and Paolo Procaccioli (eds.) *Cum notibusse et commentaribusse: l'esegisi parodistica e giocosa del Cinquecento* (Rome, 2002); Longhi, *Lusus*; Martine Boiteux, 'Chasse aux taureaux et jeux romains à la Renaissance', in Ariès and Margolin (eds.) *Les jeux*, 33–54; Domenico Scafoglio, *Il carnevale napolitano* (Rome, 1997); Horst Bredekamp,

Play in Renaissance Italy

These contributions have more to say than their predecessors about the social and cultural contexts for different forms of play. Given the increasing number of histories of emotions, a promising direction for future research, inspired by Norbert Elias on 'the quest for excitement', might be the emotions triggered by play, from joy to anger – the anger of losers at a game of dice, for instance, or the anger of the victims of practical jokes. Mock-fighting often turned into serious fighting, as we shall see. Competition in play offered many occasions of anger, as latent aggression rose to the surface.

What is still lacking is an overview that links different specialisms. Such an overview is all the more necessary because innovations in one branch of play were sometimes inspired by innovations in another. It becomes easier to understand each genre or medium of play when its connections with other genres and media are viewed as part of a bigger picture. This essay offers a sketch for such a picture.

Florentiner Fussball (Frankfurt, 1993); Alessandra Rizzi, *Ludus/ludere: giocare in Italia alla fine del medio evo* (Rome, 1995), 89–102, 171–204.

2
Fun and Games

This chapter offers descriptions of the many and various games – in a wide sense of that term – that were played in Renaissance Italy. The sources for reconstructing these games are much richer than they are for the Middle Ages, including treatises on games in general and also on specific activities such as chess, dancing, football and tennis. Some of the treatises were widely read. By the year 1609, Girolamo Bargagli's *Dialogo dei Giuochi* (first published in 1572) had been reprinted eight times.[1]

Some of the most important of these treatises were produced not in Florence, Rome or Venice but in three smaller cities: Ferrara, Siena and Bologna. In Ferrara, the rulers and the courtiers seem to have taken a particular

---

[1] Innocentio Ringhieri, *Cento giochi liberali* (Bologna, 1550); Annibale Romei, 'Le fatiche sopra il gioco degli scacchi' (manuscript written c. 1565); Girolamo Bargagli, *Dialogo dei Giuochi* (1572: ed. Patrizia Ermini, Siena, 1982); Torquato Tasso, *Del giocho* (two dialogues, written 1581-2); Scipione Bargagli, *Trattenimenti* (1587: ed. Laura Riccò, Rome, 1989). Cf. John McClelland, 'Sport and Scientific Thinking in the Sixteenth Century: Ruling Out Playfulness', *Ludica* 19–20 (2013–14), 134–45.

interest in different forms of play. The Duke, Alfonso II, was particularly interested in ball games, sometimes keeping envoys waiting while he was playing.[2] A treatise on *palla* (an ancestor of tennis), formulating rules, was written for Alfonso by a diplomat in his service, the priest Antonio Scaino.[3] Scaino gave the game an underpinning in philosophy, including natural philosophy. In Siena, the initiative appears to have come from academies, a favourite form of sociability for urban elites. The Bargagli brothers, for instance, were both members of the Sienese Academy of the *Intronati*.

The invention of printing was doubtless an encouragement to individuals with some kind of expertise in this ample domain to set down their knowledge and ideas in writing. It is likely that the treatises not only described rules for different games but also constructed them, or at the very least helped – like grammars of vernacular languages – to standardize practices that had previously varied from one place to another.

Outdoor Games[4]

In a few cases, the forms of play were shaped by the humanist project of reviving classical antiquity. The

---

[2] Andreas Hermann Fischer, *Spielen und Philosophieren zwischen Spätmittelalter und Früher Neuzeit* (Göttingen, 2016), 227.

[3] Antonio Scaino, *Trattato del giuocho della palla* (1555: English translation, *Scaino on Tennis*, London, 1951). On him, Fischer, *Spielen und Philosophieren*, 213–51; Cees de Bondt, 'Antonio Scaino's *Trattato del giuoco della palla*', *Ludica* 24 (2018), 7–19. Cf. Stefan Grössing, 'Pallone: ein aristokratisches Ballspiel', *Homo Ludens* 6 (1996), 79–105; Cees de Bondt, *Royal Tennis in Renaissance Italy* (Turnhout, 2006); Franco Pignatti, '*Antonfrancesco Grazzini: capitolo sul gioco del pallone*', *Ludica* (2010) 15–16, 167–72.

[4] Alessandra Rizzi, 'L'attività fisica', and 'Pro bravio sive palio correndo',

Fun and Games

practice of athletics was revived by following the Greek example. In the fifteenth century, the many-sided Leonbattista Alberti recommended exercise and prided himself on his jumping, while a later humanist, Girolamo Mercuriale, published a book on *The Art of Gymnastics* (1569). Nevertheless, the outdoor games of the Renaissance owed much more to medieval traditions than they did to classical models.

For the nobility, the most important forms of exercise were riding, hunting and practice in the use of weapons, especially lances and swords. Young nobles went to fencing schools. They practised their horsemanship by 'riding at the ring' (piercing a ring with a lance while galloping), or by 'riding at the quintain', spearing a life-sized doll, known in Italian as a 'Saracen'. Martial games were viewed as training for war, as well as a means to show off one's courage and skill to impress the ladies and 'cut a good figure' *(fare bella figura)*, as Italians still say.[5] Hunting, a favourite pursuit of the upper classes in Italy, as elsewhere, was also justified as training for war. In the fourteenth chapter of *The Prince*, for instance, Machiavelli wrote that 'Hunting is excellent exercise, because it strengthens the body and makes the ruler more familiar with the surrounding terrain.' Falconry was another noble sport.

Jousts – in which an individual armed with a blunted lance tried to knock his opponent off his horse – and tournaments, a form of mock-battle with real weapons, remained common practices in the fifteenth and early

in *Ludus/ludere: giocare in Italia alla fine del medio evo* (Rome, 1995), 89–102, 171–204.
[5] Sydney Anglo, *The Martial Arts of Renaissance Europe* (New Haven, CT, 2000).

sixteenth centuries. Lorenzo de' Medici, for instance, the unofficial ruler of Florence from 1469 to 1492, won first prize in a joust there in the year in which he came to power, an event celebrated by the poet Luigi Pulci in his 'Stanzas for the Joust' (*Stanze per la Giostra*). The prowess of Lorenzo's younger brother Giuliano in a joust on Piazza Santa Croce in 1475 was celebrated by a poem with the same title as Pulci's, written by the humanist Angelo Poliziano.[6] These competitive games had – among other things – the serious purpose of showing that the mercantile family of the Medici had accepted the noble values known as chivalry and were therefore fit to govern.

Only in the later sixteenth century, when the use of guns was transforming warfare, did jousts and tournaments turn into a kind of choreography – so many displays of the elegance and grace recommended in Castiglione's *Book of the Courtier*.[7] An even more spectacular display was the mock sea battle, or *naumachia*, following classical models, which was staged in the courtyard of the Pitti Palace in Florence, flooded for the purpose during the celebration of the wedding of Grand Duke Ferdinando de' Medici and Christine of Lorraine in 1589.

Tournaments and jousts were joined by football (*calcio*) and tennis (*pallone*), games that were mainly – though not exclusively – played by upper-class males. In Florence, a ball game was played on Piazza Santa Croce, following a ritual defiance that gave the game

[6] Lucia Ricciardi, *Col senno, col tesoro e colla lancia: riti e giochi cavallereschi nella Firenze del Magnifico Lorenzo* (Florence, 1992).
[7] Sandra Cavallo and Tessa Storey, *Healthy Living in Late Renaissance Italy* (Oxford, 2013), 159.

Fun and Games

Figure 1 *Calcio Fiorentino* 1688
Source: Wikimedia Commons

something of the atmosphere of a tournament.[8] In *pallone*, an ancestor of tennis, the ball was struck either by the palm of the hand, by a glove, by a wooden cylinder worn over the forearm, or by a racquet.

Mock-battles were not a preserve of the Italian nobility. At a lower social level, on foot rather than on horseback, were what is known as the 'little battles' (*battagliole*). The most famous or notorious of these battles were the 'fist wars' (*guerre de' pugni*) or 'stick wars' (*guerre de' canne*), regularly waged between the inhabitants of two quarters of Venice: the Castellani, who worked on ship-building at the Arsenal, and the Nicolotti, mainly fishermen.[9] Battles usually took place on the borders of

---

[8] Horst Bredekamp, *Florentiner Fussball* (Frankfurt, 1993).
[9] Robert C. Davis, *The War of the Fists: Popular Culture and Public Violence in Late Renaissance Venice* (New York, 1994).

their territories, especially bridges, liminal spaces appropriate for rituals of solidarity among the community of each quarter.[10] Bones might be broken, but communal bonds were mended. The encounters were celebrated in a poem by the goldsmith Alessandro Caravia, 'The Old War' (*La verra antiga*, 1550).

In similar fashion, in Florence, there were battles on the bridge of Santa Trinità which separated the quarters of Santa Maria Novella and Santo Spirito, while, in Pisa, an annual battle known as 'the bridge game' (*il gioco del ponte*) took place on the Ponte Vecchio and once again pitted men from rival quarters against each other.[11] Elsewhere, the two sides threw stones at each other, as was the tradition in Perugia, for instance.[12] These battles may appear to be huge brawls, free-for-alls, but there were what might be called 'rules of disorder', implicit in the case of Venice but explicit in that of Pisa.[13] Less formal were snowball fights, which are rarely recorded but seem to have appealed to all classes and both sexes.

Another popular exercise was the race or *palio* ('banner'), named after the prize awarded to the winner. The *palio* is still run in Siena. In the summary description of the American folklorist Alan Dundes, 'Twice a summer, for approximately 90 seconds, ten horses race clockwise three times around the Piazza del Campo, the main square of the city of Siena, which has been trans-

---

[10] On liminality, Victor Turner, *The Forest of Symbols* (Ithaca, NY, 1964), 93–111.
[11] Luigi Giovannini, *Notizie storiche sul giuoco del ponte di Pisa* (Florence, 1906).
[12] Mauro Menichelli, *La battaglia dei sassi di Perugia* (Perugia, 2001).
[13] Davis, *The War of the Fists*, 48. I have borrowed a phrase from the title of a study of British football hooligans: Peter Marsh, Elizabeth Rosser and Rom Harré, *The Rules of Disorder* (London, 1978).

formed into a race track for the occasion. The horses are ridden bareback by jockeys wearing costumes displaying the colours of ten of Siena's seventeen *contrade* or wards.' In the period with which this essay is concerned, the race used to take place through the city rather than in its centre, while the mounts were buffaloes and asses, replaced by horses in 1633.[14]

The *palio* of Siena was only one of many such races held in different Italian cities in the Middle Ages. In Venice, during Carnival, there were boat races along the Grand Canal and bull races across the bridge at the Rialto. In Florence, the *palio* of San Giovanni was a horse race that took place on 24 June, during the festival of the patron of the city. Originally intended to encourage civic patriotism by commemorating the victories of the commune, it was reduced to 'a mere competitive sport' by the fifteenth century.[15] In Rome, there were races of buffaloes and asses during Carnival, while Paul II, who was Pope from 1464 to 1471, introduced foot races along the Via Lata (hence its new name, the Corso). The events included races by Jews, prostitutes and old men. Although the winner of each race was rewarded, the participants are unlikely to have enjoyed the races, which offered the bystanders opportunities to throw stones and shout insults.[16]

Other games offered displays of skill by professionals. Acrobatics, for example, required rigorous training. In Venice, the displays included tightrope walking and

[14] Alan Dundes and Alessandro Falassi, *La Terra in Piazza: An Interpretation of the Palio of Siena* (Berkeley, CA, 1975), xi.
[15] Rizzi, *Ludus*, 197, 202.
[16] Alessandro Ademollo, *Il carnevale di Roma* (Rome, 1883); Martine Boiteux, 'Les Juifs dans le Carnaval de Rome moderne', *Mélanges de l'École Française de Rome* (1976), 745–87.

the human pyramid known as 'the forces of Hercules' (*le forze d'Ercole*).¹⁷ Some mock-battles were a kind of outdoor theatre, as in the case of festive sieges of castles, like the one in Florence in 1513 described in a contemporary chronicle.

Battles between animals presented a kind of 'theatre of cruelty'. Watching two cocks fighting was a common sport in Italy. 'Bear-baiting', in which the bear was attacked by dogs, was another common sport in Italy, as in early modern England. So was bullfighting, the *caccia tori*: Cesare Borgia, the son of the Spanish Pope Alexander VI, sometimes took part, while a battle between men and bulls on Rome's Piazza Farnese is represented in a print of the 1530s. Bulls and bears, together with lions and leopards, were hunted on the main squares of cities during festivals. The references to these occasions in local chronicles say little about the danger to spectators.

Dancing, for both men and women, was linked to festivals, notably weddings and Carnival, and took place both indoors and outdoors, at court and on the piazza. A number of treatises on dancing were published in Renaissance Italy, and the repertoire of dances was extended. For example, the traditional *moresca*, *saltarella* and *tripudio* were joined by the *gagliardo*, a lively dance that became fashionable, as the 'galliard', in Elizabethan England, where the courtier Sir Christopher Hatton is said to have danced his way into the queen's favour. It was in Italy in the fifteenth century that court

---

[17] Antonella Fenech Kroke, 'Giochi acrobatici', in Francesca Aceto and Francesco Lucioli (eds.) *Giocare tra Medioevo ed età moderna* (Treviso and Rome, 2019), 37–60.

dances began to be separated from popular dances, part of a slow but significant withdrawal of the European upper classes from participation in popular culture. Certain dances were becoming symbols of civility and courtly manners.[18]

Dancing reminds us that music was – and still is – a form of recreation. It is no accident that we, like the Italians of the Renaissance, speak of 'playing' the piano or the guitar (or, in their case, the harpsichord or the lute). Listening, too, was a form of recreation, and dances, festivals, plays and the performances of singers of tales were all accompanied by music. All the same, compared with our own time, music, especially singing, was mainly a form of 'do it yourself'. There are many references, both in archives and in the accounts of travellers, to singing in the street. The publication of sheet music was followed by the rise of songs for a number of voices. In the fifteenth century, the popular genres were the *frottola* and the *strambotto*, usually for four voices, replaced in the sixteenth century by the madrigal.[19]

Music was also the vehicle for other forms of play. For example, the *villanesca* or *villanella*, a name that linked the genre to rustics (*villani*), was a form of song for three voices that originated in Naples and spread to Rome and other places. It was sung in Neapolitan dialect and the words often played on the double meanings

---

[18] Nanie Bridgman, *La vie musicale au quattrocento* (Paris, 1964), 62; Alessandro Arcangeli, 'Dance in the Sixteenth Century', *Ludica* 19–20 (2013–14), 173–81. On the withdrawal of the upper classes, Peter Burke, *Popular Culture in Early Modern Europe* (1978: 3rd edn, Farnham, 2009), 366–80.

[19] Bridgman, *La vie musicale*, 149–58; Alfred Einstein, *The Italian Madrigal* (1949: revised edn, 3 vols., Princeton, NJ, 2019).

so common in the comedies, dialogues, verses and even the visual culture of this period.[20] At a more sophisticated level, the French composer Josquin des Prez, who spent most of his career in Italy, imitated the sound of the cricket in the song 'The cricket is a good singer' (*Il grillo e buon cantore*).

Playful music was associated with Roland de Lassus in particular – a Netherlander who worked in many parts of Italy and was known there as Orlando Lasso. A polyglot who loved wordplay in five languages, as his letters show, Lassus produced not only settings for bawdy and other comic songs (including *villanelle*) but also the musical equivalent of puns, imitating everyday sounds. He also improvised a comedy at the court of Munich in which he acted, sang madrigals and played the accompaniment.[21] In the comedies of Orazio Vecchi and Adriano Banchieri, the story was told in madrigals.[22]

Indoor Games

While outdoor games were mainly for men, indoor games were mainly for women and also for mixed company, offering as they did various opportunities for flirtation. The most famous indoor games of the Renaissance are surely those represented in two classic

---

[20] Donna G. Cardamone, 'Erotic Jest and Gesture in Roman Anthologies of Neapolitan Dialect Songs', *Music and Letters* 86 (2005), 357–79.

[21] Frank Langlois (ed.) *Con bien fou tu serais Orlando: correspondance de Roland de Lassus avec le prince de Bavière* (Arles, 1988); Annie Coeurdevey, 'Roland de Lassus ou l'invention de l'humour en musique', in Marie Madeleine Fontaine (ed.) *Rire à la Renaissance* (Geneva, 2010), 257–72; Roberto Tessari, *La Commedia dell'arte* (Rome, 2013), 27, 91.

[22] Martha Farahat, 'On the Staging of Madrigal Comedies', *Early Music History* 10 (1991), 123–43.

Fun and Games

texts, Boccaccio's *Decameron* and Castiglione's *Book of the Courtier*. Each is supposed to have been improvised on a particular occasion.

In the case of the *Decameron*, a collection of stories told in the course of ten days, the occasion was the great plague of 1348, the 'Black Death'. Seven young ladies, together with three young men, flee from Florence to a villa in the countryside. They choose a 'queen', who decides that to entertain themselves in their isolation they will take turns to tell stories.

As for the *Book of the Courtier*, it is presented by the author both as a 'portrait' of the court of Urbino and as the record of a discussion that took place there after dinner over four evenings in 1507, two decades before his dialogue was published. As in the *Decameron*, the group of ladies and gentlemen chooses a leader, the Lady Emilia, who in turn decides that they will pass the time by discussing the qualities of the perfect courtier. The conversation is presented as a 'game' (*gioco*), and its participants as laughing (*ridendo*) as they listen to the speeches. One of the gentlemen, Gaspare Pallavicino, likes to tease the ladies, and they tease him in return. Castiglione's dialogue offers us a fine example of the art of playing seriously, *giocare serio*.[23]

Boccaccio and Castiglione both present the games they describe as spontaneous, invented on the spur of the moment. In the course of the period, however, indoor games multiplied and so did their rules. Contemporaries distinguished between two main categories, 'games of

---

[23] Thomas M. Greene, '*Il Cortegiano* and the Choice of a Game', in R. W. Hanning and David Rosand (eds.) *Castiglione: The Ideal and the Real in Renaissance Culture* (New Haven, CT, 1983), 1–16.

chance' (*giochi d'azzardo*), and 'liberal games' (*giochi liberali*), and I shall follow this classification here. Rolling dice and betting on the result was a widespread practice that went back to the ancient world and had the advantage that it could be played anywhere, even in church (as we know from reiterated prohibitions). It was suspect to the authorities of both the Church and the city because it offered occasions of sin (including blasphemy by the losers), as well as for brawls. Like the cock-fight in Bali, famously analysed by the anthropologist Clifford Geertz, it was an example of what he called 'deep play', because 'much more is at stake than material gain'.[24] Loss meant loss of face or, as Italians still say, *fare brutta figura*. 'Face' was important at this time, when affirming or defending one's status was a constant preoccupation, as the many conflicts over precedence in church or in processions make abundantly clear. Losing to someone who was perceived as a social inferior was particularly galling. In playing a game with a prince, whether it was tennis or chess, it was advisable to let him win.

Among other games of chance, card games were popular at this time, and the mass-production of playing cards by printers helped them to spread both geographically and socially.[25] The term *Trionfi* for a kind of card game is recorded in 1440. *Tarocchi* was a game with tarot cards, mentioned in 1505 (it was only in the eighteenth century that these cards were regularly used to

---

[24] Clifford Geertz, 'Deep Play', in *The Interpretation of Cultures* (New York, 1973), 412–53.
[25] Gherardo Ortalli, 'The Prince and the Playing Cards', *Ludica* (1996); Ortalli, *Barattieri: il gioco d'azzardo fra economia ed etica. Secoli XIII–XV* (Bologna, 2012); Ortalli (ed.) *Lotteries, Lotto, Slot Machines. The Luck of the Draw: A History of Games of Chance* (Treviso, 2019).

tell fortunes). In 1513, Machiavelli described himself as playing *Cricca*, a game where the aim is to accumulate three of a kind. *Primero* was an ancestor of poker, in which players might bluff by overstating the strength of their hands. The first reference to the game dates from 1526. In *Bassetta*, another sixteenth-century game, the players had to guess in whose pile a particular card would appear. Another early reference is to *Trappola*, the first trick-taking game: its rules were described by the mathematician-physician Girolamo Cardano in his book on games of chance.[26] The writer Pietro Aretino's *Le carte parlanti* (1543) described a variety of card games with comments in his usual style, mixing wit with both malice and morality.[27]

Giochi liberali or *giochi di sala*, known later as 'parlour games', also flourished in Renaissance Italy. Some were guessing games (*giochi da indovinare*), others were known by the general name of 'intellectual games' or 'games of wit' (*giochi d'ingegno, giochi di spirito*). Several guides to the rules of these games were published in this period: Lorenzo Spirto's *Libro della Ventura* (1476), for instance, which used three dice to answer twenty questions, a book that had appeared in nineteen editions by 1557; Sigismondo Fonti's *Triompho di Fortuna* (1527), which offered answers to seventy-two questions by a progression through 'fortunes, houses, wheels,

---

[26] Girolamo Cardano, *De ludo aleae* (c. 1564: English translation, *The Book on Games of Chance*, New York, 1961), section 25; Oystein Ore, *Cardano, the Gambling Scholar* (Princeton, NJ, 1953); Giovanni Dolcetti, *Le bische e il giuoco d'azzardo a Venezia, 1172–1807* (Venice, 1903); Michael Dummett, *A History of Games Played with the Tarot Pack* (Oxford, 2004).

[27] Paolo Procaccioli, '"Così fan tutti": Le carte "parlanti" di Pietro Aretino', *Ludica* 19–20 (2013–14), 106–16.

spheres and astrologers' (*fortune, case, rote, sphere,* and *astrologi*); Francesco Marcolini's *Le ingeniose sorti* (1540), which used cards to select the answers to various questions; Innocentio Ringhieri's encyclopaedic *Cento giochi liberali* (1550); and Girolamo Bargagli's *Dialogo dei Giuochi* (1572). Since Ringhieri included 100 games, Bargagli had to overtake him and included 130. The spread of all these games was assisted once again by the rise of printing, not only of the guides that explained the sometimes complicated rules, but also of texts that players might need during the game itself.[28]

Some of the most common of games of wit were what we know as 'board games'. Chess, which was of course played long before the Renaissance, was the subject of a poem by the humanist bishop Girolamo Vida, *Scacchia ludus* (1527), in which he describes Apollo playing against Mercury. The game, formerly a leisurely one, was speeded up by changes in the rules in the late sixteenth century.[29] Draughts, known as 'the game of the lady' (*gioco della dama*), was also played in Italy. Another well-known game was *Tric-Trac*, more or less what we know as 'backgammon', which Niccolò Machiavelli regularly played with butchers and bakers in his local tavern when he was exiled from Florence in 1513, before going home in the evening to write another chapter of *The Prince*. *Biribissi* was a board game like the modern bingo, in which the players betted on a cer-

---

[28] Thomas F. Crane, 'Parlor Games', in *Italian Social Customs of the Sixteenth Century* (New Haven, CT, 1920), ch. 6; Roberta Lencioni Novelli, 'Un trattato in forma di giuoco', in *Passare il tempo* (Rome, 1993), 691–706; George McClure, *Parlour Games and the Public Life of Women in Renaissance Italy* (Toronto, 2013).
[29] H. J. R. Murray, *A History of Chess* (Oxford, 1913), 224–6.

tain number coming up. *Pela il chiu* ('pluck the owl'), described as a 'new' game in 1589, was played with dice and counters. It was an ancestor of 'snakes and ladders'.

Guessing games (*giochi da indovinare*) appealed especially to women, at least according to the courtier Annibale Romei. They included fortune-telling, with the help of the 'Book of Chance' by Lorenzo Gualtieri, a text first published in 1482 and reprinted at least eleven times; the 'Triumph of Fortune' of the mathematician Sigismondo Fonti (1526); and the 'Fortunes' (1540) by the Venetian bookseller Francesco Marcolini.[30] Whether or not the fortunes revealed were taken seriously is difficult to say.

Quizzes were already a common form of game, particularly ones that tested the players' knowledge of the poems of Petrarch and Ariosto and the stories of Boccaccio (Dante was mentioned much less frequently). Treatises on games are full of quotations from these authors, and references to the names of characters in the *Decameron* and *Orlando Furioso*.[31] Other games offered opportunities for demonstrating skill in argument, as in the 'game of the ship' (no relation of the video game of the same title), in which the lady has to decide which of two men she must throw overboard, while they have

---

[30] Lorenzo Gualtieri (nicknamed 'Spirito'), *Libro della Ventura* (Bologna, 1482); Sigismondo Fonti, *Triunfo della Fortuna* (1526); Francesco Marcolini, *Le Sorti* (Venice, 1540; repr. Treviso and Rome, 2007). Cf. Paolo Procaccioli (ed.) *Studi per le 'Sorti'* (Treviso, 2007), and Fischer, *Spielen und Philosophieren*, 161–4 (on Marcolini).

[31] François Lecercle, 'La culture en jeu: Innocenzo Ringhieri et le Pétrarquisme', and Riccardo Brusceglia, 'Les Intronati "a Veglia"', in Philippe Ariès and Jean-Claude Margolin (eds.) *Les jeux à la Renaissance* (Paris, 1982), 185–200 and 201–12, respectively. References to Petrarch and Ariosto abound in the texts of Ringhieri and Girolamo Bargagli.

to offer convincing arguments for remaining. It is the ancestor of later 'balloon debates'.[32]

Another favourite game was inventing *imprese*, devices that combined an enigmatic image with a motto, and sometimes a quatrain which, when itself decoded, would explain the meaning of the image.[33] Enigmas of this kind, together with riddles, were Renaissance equivalents of the later crossword puzzle. Girolamo Bargagli's *Dialogo dei Giuochi* includes one that requires the player to devise such an *impresa* for the reverse of a medal, while his younger brother Scipione wrote on *imprese* as well as on games. Players were recommended to seek inspiration in a treatise on ancient Roman medals, thus offering an example, as did gymnastics, of the influence of the revival of antiquity on the world of play. Mathematical problems might be viewed as games. Leonbattista Alberti's collection of problems was entitled 'Mathematical Games' (*ludi mathematici*).

Competition

As the French theorist Roger Caillois emphasized, many forms of play depend on competition. Gambling on the results of games, from cock-fighting to chess, as well as dice and cards, was widespread at all social levels.[34] The

---

[32] Bargagli, *Dialogo*, game no. 49, 'della Nave'. There is now a video game entitled 'The Ship', https://en.wikipedia.org/wiki/The_Ship.

[33] Kristen Lippincott, 'The Genesis and Significance of the Fifteenth-Century Italian *Impresa*', in Sydney Anglo (ed.) *Chivalry in the Renaissance* (Woodbridge, 1990), 49–76.

[34] Dolcetti, *Le bische e il giuoco d'azzardo a Venezia*; Jonathan Walker, 'Gambling and Venetian Noblemen, c. 1500–1700', *Past and Present* 162 (1999), 28–69.

money was only part of the pleasure of winning and the shame of losing. It was 'status gambling' as well as 'money gambling'. Money mattered too: competing for prizes of money included the *lotto*, a lottery with numbered tickets.[35]

Gambling was only one form of competitive play, while play was only one form of competition. Like ancient Greece, Renaissance Italy was an 'agonistic culture'. As Jacob Burckhardt emphasized in his lectures on the cultural history of Greece, the ancient Greeks were extremely competitive. The *Iliad* already notes their urge 'always to be the first and outdo all the others'. They institutionalized this desire to win, first in chariot-races and then in gymnastics, especially the famous Olympic Games, with prizes to commemorate victors and victories.[36] In *Homo Ludens*, Johan Huizinga, a historian who both admired and criticized Burckhardt's work, praised his emphasis on the agonistic element in Greek culture.[37]

In Renaissance Italy, competition in trade is obvious enough. In the cases of sculpture and architecture, competition for commissions was institutionalized. In Florence in 1401, for instance, the goldsmith Lorenzo Ghiberti defeated the polymath Filippo Brunelleschi and won the commission to make the bronze doors for the Baptistery. Competition took place not only between

---

[35] Geertz, 'Deep Play', 433, 435; Achille Olivieri, 'Jeu et capitalisme à Venise', in Ariès and Margolin (eds.) *Les jeux*, 151–62.
[36] Jacob Burckhardt, *The Greeks and Greek Civilization*, ed. Oswyn Murray (London, 1998), 160–213 (a selection from Burckhardt's posthumously published lecture notes).
[37] Johan Huizinga, *Homo Ludens: A Study of the Play Element in Culture* (1938: English translation, 2nd edn, London, 1970), 92.

individuals but also between parishes and quarters (think of the 'fist wars'), between guilds and between cities. The tower of the Palazzo Pubblico in Siena, the town hall, was built deliberately higher than the tower of its equivalent in Florence, the Palazzo della Signoria. The Sienese would surely have appreciated the motto of Avis, the second-largest car rental company in the USA in 1962: 'We Try Harder.'

The many literary feuds recorded in Renaissance Italy may be interpreted in terms of competition. Gifted writers, often of low birth and short of money, jostled for a place at the table of a patron, bad-mouthing their actual and possible rivals and using their verbal skills to destroy their enemies with the weapon of ridicule: Francesco Berni and Antonfranceso Doni versus Pietro Aretino, Annibale Caro versus Lodovico Castelvetro, Alfonso de' Pazzi versus Benedetto Varchi. Verbal violence will be discussed in more detail in the following chapter.

In the second book of Alberti's dialogue on the family, one speaker, Leonardo, having evoked the games described by Virgil in the *Aeneid*, described life as a race – in this case, a boat race – in which it is necessary 'to sweat to be first' (*sudare di essere il primo*) in the competition for honour.[38] In the next century, the famous handbook of good manners, the *Galateo*, a posthumously published work by the Florentine Archbishop Giovanni Della Casa (1503–56), warned readers not to be carried away by 'the sweetness of winning' (*la dol-*

---

[38] Leonbattista Alberti, *I libri della famiglia*, ed. Ruggiero Romano and Alberto Tenenti (Turin, 1969), 167–8.

cezza del vincere).[39] No wonder then that there was so much competition in the sphere of games. The winner had the dangerous pleasure of dominating, humiliating or even ruining the loser. As we shall see in the following chapter, humiliating rivals was also a major theme or motive in the domain of laughter.

---

[39] Giovanni Della Casa, *Il Galateo* (1558: ed. Dino Provenzal, Milan, 1950), ch. 18.

3
Laughter

Readers of this chapter may discover that what passed for humour in Renaissance Italy, even in the most sophisticated milieu of the court, does not seem funny to them at all. This is a common problem: many jokes do not travel well between cultures or between centuries. For that very reason, what is considered to be humorous in a given place, time and milieu offers outsiders, such as historians or anthropologists, a key to understanding that particular culture.

For example, at the court of Urbino, as described in Castiglione's *Courtier*, pellets of bread were thrown at table. Practical jokes were common at all levels of society. Dwarves (*nani*) had a place in Renaissance courts because they were figures of fun. A speaker in Castiglione's *Courtier*, Bernardo da Bibbiena, explained (following Cicero) that the perception of physical deformity is a common cause of laughter. Reacting against this idea, Giovanni Della Casa's guide to good manners, the *Galateo* (1558), warned readers against imitating stutterers, lame people and hunchbacks.[1] It may still be necessary to warn children or adolescents about throwing bread or imitating stutterers, but the cultural gap between children and adults was not so great in the Renaissance as it is now, while the discovery – or, perhaps, the 'invention' – of adolescence had not yet taken place.

Castiglione's dialogue is probably the best-known contribution to what might be called the Renaissance theory of laughter, discussing why people laugh and what is worthy of laughter. Keeping close to spoken language, the author performed what he discussed, allowing his characters to make fun of one another. Gasparo Pallavicino, for instance, regularly teases the ladies, and they gang up on him for their revenge. Printed dialogues were a major form of literature at this time. Some of them, like the *Book of the Courtier*, exemplify the art of playing seriously, notably 'The Ash Wednesday Supper' (1584, *La cena delle ceneri*) by the unorthodox philosopher Giordano Bruno, in which even the title is a play on words (*La cena delle ceneri*), and Galileo's *Dialogue on the Two Main World Systems* (1632), in which the defender of Aristotle and Ptolemy, Simplicio, is made into a figure of fun.[2]

Renissance theories of the comic include contributions by the humanists Giovanni Pontano, Vincenzo Maggi and Lodovico Castelvetro.[3] As in other fields

---

[1] Baldassare Castiglione, *Il Cortegiano* (1528: ed. Bruno Maier, Turin, 1964), book 2, section 46; Giovanni Della Casa, *Il Galateo* (1558: ed. Dino Provenzal, Milan, 1950), ch.19.

[2] Paula Findlen's forthcoming study, 'Galileo's Laughter: Knowledge and Play in the Renaissance', promises to discuss this question in detail and depth.

[3] Giovanni Pontano, *De sermone* (ed. Alessandra Mantovani, Rome, 2002); Ernst Walzer, *Die Theorie des Witzes nach Jovianus Pontanus* (Strasbourg,

at this time, the humanists did not stray very far from two ancient authorities, one Greek and one Roman: Aristotle and Cicero, both of whom discussed humour and wit in their treatises on oratory. Pontano, writing in Latin and coining a new term for a joke, *facetudo*, praised the individual whose conversation is humorous, urbane and witty (*facetus, festivus, salsus*), while avoiding unpleasantness or buffoonery.

If the upper classes were beginning to look down on buffoonery in the sixteenth century, many other people continued to admire buffoons and to laugh at their antics. The 'Tricks of Bertoldo' (*Astuzie di Bertoldo*), published in 1620 by the prolific popular poet Giulio Cesare Croce of Bologna, has been described as a masterpiece of the 'carnivalesque literature' of the period, creating the character of a comic but cunning peasant.[4]

Wordplay

Johan Huizinga, who wrote on the Renaissance as well as on *Homo ludens*, argued that 'the whole mental attitude of the Renaissance was one of play' and that 'We would be hard put to it to name a poet who embodies the play-spirit more purely than Ariosto.'[5] The leading humanists of the Renaissance clearly loved what they called *facezie, motti* and *arguzie* (in other words, jokes

---

1908); Amedeo Quondam, *La conversazione: un modello Italiano* (Rome, 2011), 55–61; Juan Carlos Pueo, *Ridens et ridiculus: Vincenzo Maggi y la teoría humanista de la risa* (Zaragoza, 2001).
[4] Piero Camporesi, *La maschera di Bertoldo: G. C. Croce e la letteratura carnevalesca* (Turin, 1976).
[5] Johan Huizinga, *Homo Ludens: A Study of the Play Element in Culture* (1938: English translation, 2nd edn, London, 1970), 206.

and witticisms). They collected them into jestbooks, some of which were published at the time. The roll-call includes the poet Petrarch, Poggio Bracciolini, Agnolo Poliziano and Pietro Bembo. Other jestbooks were produced in the name of the priest Arlotto Mainardi, and the writer, translator and compiler Lodovico Domenichi.[6] As both the theorists and the collections show, two qualities of jests were particularly appreciated. In the first place, *prontezza* – in other words, verbal agility, a rapid response to provocation, a gift for repartee, smacking the ball back at the adversary. Secondly, jests should be 'biting' (*mordace*). The problem was to establish the limits, the point at which a joke became an insult that needed a response in action rather than words. In the words that Castiglione attributed to his friend Bibbiena, jokes should not 'give offence and strike at the heart' (*far dispetto e dar nel core*).[7] Della Casa agreed, distinguishing the *motti* that 'bite' from the ones that do not. In short, *allegro, ma non troppo*.[8]

Stories, poems and songs often refer to what Bakhtin described euphemistically as the 'lower bodily stratum', especially the genitals and the sexual act. They employ a rich variety of vivid metaphors such as figs, noses, sausages, frying pans, ploughing the soil and turning a key in the lock. The poet Francesco Berni, known in his day as the 'master and father of the burlesque style', showed amazing virtuosity in this domain, but

---

[6] On Poggio, Lionel Sozzi, 'Les facéties du Pogge et leur influence', *Bulletin de l'Association d'étude sur l'humanisme, la réforme et la renaissance* 7 (1977), 31–5. For a full list, see Barbara C. Bowen, 'Renaissance Collections of Facetiae', *Renaissance Quarterly* 39 (1986), 1–15, 263–75.
[7] Castiglione, *Il Cortegiano*, book 2, section 57.
[8] Della Casa, *Il Galateo*, ch. 20.

there was plenty of competition. In his youth, the future Archbishop Giovanni Della Casa composed five comic poems 'as a joke' (*per jocum*), as he confessed later. One was entitled *Bacio* (which, as in today's French, meant more than a kiss), and another, *Forno* ('oven' – where the double meaning of 'putting a bun in the oven' has survived in today's English).[9] Freud would have appreciated the variety of the metaphors, in which a wide range of everyday objects (mortars and pestles, swords and sheaths, and so on) were all pressed into the service of sexual allusion. As the French scholar Jean Toscan, who devoted three volumes of his doctoral dissertation to the subject, has pointed out, there is a striking contrast between the richness of the signifiers (the system of metaphors), and the poverty of the signified – little more than buttocks, penis and vagina.

Wordplay in its different forms, from puns to parody, exists in many cultures and periods, but it seems to have been particularly appreciated at this time. It was a way of showing – and showing off – the ingenuity so much prized in the culture of the Renaissance. The painter Michelangelo da Caravaggio could not resist calling his enemy Giovanni Baglione – another artist – *Coglione* ('balls'). Nonsense verses about 'fried nouns' and 'hunchbacked pumpkins' made the fifteenth-century Florentine barber Domenico di Giovanni, nicknamed 'Burchiello', famous in his city and an inspiration to later comic poets. A new verb, *burchielleggiare*, bears eloquent wit-

---

[9] Jean Toscan, *Le carnaval du langage*, 5 vols. (Lille, 1981), vol. I, 137–347; Antono Corsaro, 'Giovanni Della Casa e la poesia burlesca', in *La regola e la licenza: studi sulla poesia satirica e burlesca fra cinque e seicento* (Rome, 1999), 73–113.

ness to his success.[10] To be 'copious' – finding different ways of saying the same thing, never using one word when six will do – was a quality much prized at this time, and the prolific Pietro Aretino offers a supreme example of this facility, as we shall see.

Linguistic virtuosity included mixing languages or dialects, a staple device of comedy. Italians were the pioneers of what is known as 'macaronic' verse, in which a vernacular vocabulary was combined with Latin syntax. Probably invented by students at the University of Padua, the masterpiece in this genre is surely *Baldus* (1517), a mock-epic by a former monk, Teofilo Folengo.[11]

Although the majority of Italians spoke in local dialects at this time, some of them found the dialects of other regions irresistibly funny. For example, the merchant poet Antonio Molino, nicknamed 'Il Burchiella', specialized in *stradiottesco*, a language based on Venetian but mixed with Croat and modern Greek and associated with professional soldiers from the Balkans, the *stradiotti*. In an anonymous comedy from the 1530s, *La Venexiana*, the women speak Venetian, the visiting foreigner speaks Tuscan and the porter speaks Bergamasque.[12] In the *commedia dell'arte*, improvised comedies that emerged in the middle of the sixteenth century and became popular both at court and in the street, an important part of

---

[10] M. Zaccarello (ed.) *La fantasia fuor de' confine: Burchiello e dintorni a 550 anni dalla morte* (Rome, 2001); Giuseppe Antonelli and Carla Chiummo (eds.) *'Nominativi fritti e mappamondi': il nonsense nella letteratura italiana* (Salerno, 2009); cf. Fabian Alfie and Aileen Feng, *The Poetry of Burchiello: Deep-Fried Nouns, Hunchbacked Pumpkins and Other Nonsense* (Tempe, AZ, 2017).

[11] Ugo E. Paoli, *Il latino maccheronico* (Florence, 1959); Ivano Paccagnella, *Le macaronee padovane* (Padua, 1979).

[12] Giorgio Padoan (ed.) *La Venexiana* (Padua, 1974).

the entertainment was provided by stylized or parodic versions of Venetian, Bolognese, Neapolitan, Paduan and Bergamasque. In Milan, a festive society presided over by the artist Gian Paolo Lomazzo chose to speak at their meetings in the language of the wine porters from a nearby valley, the Val di Bregno (in dialect, 'Blenio'). Lomazzo may be said to have combined the sublime and the bibulous. He is usually remembered for his neoplatonic theory of art, but he also wrote comic poems in dialect.[13] Giulio Cesare Croce often wrote in his native Bolognese, including the language of the *commedia dell'arte*'s 'Dottore Gratiano', but he mastered a number of other dialects as well.[14]

Literary classics such as Dante's *Divine Comedy*, Petrarch's lyrics, Ariosto's *Orlando Furioso* and Tasso's *Gerusalemme Liberata* were translated in whole or in parts into various dialects, apparently for fun rather than to reach a wider audience.[15] Translating serious poems into local dialect was a form of parody, and parody was a favourite literary genre in Renaissance Italy. Mock-epics were written in the 'comic-heroic'

---

[13] W. Theodor Elwert, 'Die mundartlichen Kunstdichtung Italiens und ihr Verhältnis zur Literatur in der Hochsprache' (1939: repr. in *Aufsätze zur italienischen Lyrik*, Wiesbaden, 1967, 156–91); James B. Lynch, 'Lomazzo and the Accademia della Valle di Bregno', *Art Bulletin* 48 (1966), 210–11; Giulio Bora, Manuela Kahn-Rossi and Francesco Porzio (eds.) *Rabisch: il grottesco nell'arte del Cinquecento. L'Accademia della Val di Blenio, Lomazzo e l'ambiente Milanese* (Milan, 1998).

[14] Camporesi, *G. C. Croce*, 97, 109–10. Cf. Elwert, 'Die mundartlichen Kunstdichtung Italiens und ihr Verhältnis zur Literatur in der Hochsprache'; Ivano Paccagnella, *Un mondo di parole: tra lingua e dialetti* (Padua, 2017).

[15] Luca D'Onghia, 'Due paragrafi sulla fortuna dialettale del "Furioso"', in Lina Bolzoni, Serena Pezzini and Giovanna Rizzarelli (eds.) *'Tra mille carte vive ancora': ricezione del 'Furioso' tra immagini e parole* (Lucca, 2010), 281–98.

Figure 2 Self-portrait of Gian Paolo Lomazzo
Source: Wikimedia Commons

style, from Folengo's *Baldus* (1517) to the 'Robbery of the Bucket' (*La Secchia Rapita*, 1622) by Alessandro Tassoni, via lesser-known works such as the companion pieces of battles of giants and dwarves, both published in 1547.[16] *Baldus* may also be regarded as a parody of the medieval romances of chivalry, in the tradition of Luigi Pulci, a poet and a diplomat at the court of Lorenzo de' Medici who wrote a narrative poem which combines the adventures of the knights Orlando and Rinaldo with those of a cast of comic characters who include the giant Morgante, from whom the poem takes its name.

A marginal case is that of Alessandro Caravia's *La verra antiga*, the poem on the 'stick wars' mentioned in the previous chapter. Right from the start, when he invokes the gods Mars and Bacchus, Caravia locates his poem in the tradition of the mock-epic, while his description of the 'pep talks' given by the leaders before the encounter parodies the orations to their armies given by generals before a battle, orations that were recurrent set pieces in the work of both ancient and Renaissance historians. However, the poet does more than simply make fun of the combatants. He also ennobles his theme by describing the battle on the bridge as a joust (*giostra*), thus claiming that honour can be won or lost by artisans and fishermen as well as by knights.[17]

The parody of the classics, ancient or modern, was the flip side of respect. It was a secular form of blasphemy, expressing the need to thumb one's nose, at least on occasion, at figures before whom one had been taught to genuflect. The Florentine pharmacist and comic writer Antonfrancesco Grazzini, defending Berni's parodies, suggested that readers were 'fed up' (*infastiditi*) with the

---

[16] By Girolamo Amelonghi and Michelangelo Serafini, respectively.
[17] Robert C. Davis, *The War of the Fists: Popular Culture and Public Violence in Late Renaissance Venice* (New York, 1994), 3, 47, 92.

classics. One comic poet, Giovanni Mauro, made fun of classical heroes and heroines such as Mutius Scaevola, Lucrezia and Regulus. Another, Jacopo Bonfadio, mocked the gods and goddesses, presenting Pluto as a baker, Diana as a washerwoman and Neptune as a fishmonger.[18] There was a comic assault on modern classicism, including *petrarcherie* and *bemberie* – in other words, the fashionable imitations of sonnets by Petrarch and his follower Pietro Bembo. Leading the assault were Berni and Aretino.[19]

Other literary genres were also parodied at this time. A particularly popular choice was the mock-encomium. An early example is Alberti's praise of the fly. The praise of figs, eels, sausages and large noses offered ample opportunities for double meanings, while poets also sang the praises of debt, hard-boiled eggs, plague, salad, syphilis, thistles, urinals and winter. The forms of parody included mock-testaments (a Carnival tradition), and mock-epitaphs or funeral sermons. Competing to compose 'ridiculous epitaphs' was the sixty-fourth game in Bargagli's collection.[20] Indeed, parody seemed to be everywhere. Giulio Cesare Croce parodied the prognostications of astrologers. The famous poem *Orlando Furioso* by Ludovico Ariosto, a nobleman at the court of Ferrara, was, among other things, an affectionate parody of the medieval romances of chivalry that contin-

---

[18] Jacopo Bonfadio, *Le lettere e una scrittura burlesca* (Rome, 1978); Maria Cristina Figorilli, 'Elogi paradossali nei due libri di *Lettere facete e piacevoli* (1561–1575)', *Italianistica* 32 (2003), 247–73, at 248, 251.

[19] Arturo Graf, 'Petrarchismo e antipetrarchismo', *Attraverso il '500* (Turin, 1926), 1–70

[20] Paolo Cherchi, 'L'encomio paradossale nel Manierismo', *Forum Italicum* 9 (1975), 368–84; Silvia Longhi, 'L'elogio paradossale', in *Lusus: il capitolo burlesco nel Cinquecento* (Padua, 1983), 138–80; Figorilli, 'Elogi'.

ued to be popular in the age of the Renaissance. Again, the dialogues (1536) by a leading comic writer, Pietro Aretino, in which an older prostitute, Nanna, advises a younger one, Pippa, on the right way to practise her profession, may be read as a 'misconduct book' – in other words, a parody of conduct books in general, and Castiglione's *Courtier* in particular. Driving the point home, Aretino dedicated three of the dialogues on the 'tricks of the trade' to a gentleman whom he described as 'an example of courtesy'.[21]

Many forms of parody can be found in other periods and other languages, but one is linked particularly closely to Renaissance Italy: the mock-commentary. This genre, inspired by ancient examples, treated modern comic texts as if they were Greek or Latin classics, discussing their grammar, the etymology of unusual words, and the different ways in which the texts might be interpreted. The humanist Annibale Caro, for instance, wrote a mock-commentary on the mock-eulogy of figs by his friend the poet Francesco Maria Molza. He played with the various meanings of *fico*, *fica*, *ficata*, *beccafico* and so on, as well as poking fun at scholars who took themselves and their learning too seriously.[22] In similar vein, Aretino located his dialogues between prostitutes under a fig tree.

---

[21] Pietro Aretino, *Sei Giornate* (1534–6: ed. Giovanni Aquilecchia, Rome-Bari, 1975), part 2.
[22] Antonio Corsaro and Paolo Procaccioli (eds.) *Cum notibusse et commentaribusse: l'esegisi parodistica e giocosa del Cinquecento* (Rome, 2002), 57–98; Danilo Romei, Michel Plaisance and Franco Pignatti, *Ludi esegetici* (Rome, 2005).

Laughter

Visual Play

It is scarcely a surprise to find that, in an age of great artists, play sometimes took visual forms. As the American scholar Paul Barolsky showed in the 1970s, at a time when jokes were not yet taken seriously by art historians, drawings, paintings and statues might all be playful.[23] In painting, as in literature, gods and classical heroes were mocked. Giovanni Bellini represented a drunken Jupiter in his *Feast of the Gods* (1514), while Tintoretto showed Vulcan the cuckold in the act of discovering his wife Venus in bed with Mars (1552). Titian parodied the famous classical sculpture *Laocoon* by representing the figures as apes, while the Lombard artist Pellegrino Tibaldi parodied Michelangelo's Sistine Chapel paintings in a fresco cycle of the *Odyssey* decorating a palace in Bologna.[24]

A different form of humour can be found in two paintings of butcher's shops by painters from Bologna from two successive generations, one by Bartolomeo Passarotti and the other by Annibale Carracci. Bartolomeo used the hanging carcasses as a symbol of sexuality, a 'visual translation' of a pun on *carne*, a word that may be translated as either 'meat' or 'flesh' (as in 'the world, the flesh and the devil'). Carracci reinforced the message by adding a dog and a ram, both common symbols of lust.[25] Another kind of visual pun was the speciality of

---

[23] Paul Barolsky, *Infinite Jest: Wit and Humor in Italian Renaissance Art* (Columbia, MO, 1978). Cf. Francesca Alberti, *La peinture facétieux* (Arles, 2016).
[24] Barolsky, *Infinite Jest*, 174, 195, 210.
[25] Barry Wind, 'Annibale Caracci's "Scherzo": The Christ Church Butcher Shop', *Art Bulletin* 58 (1976), 93–6.

the Milanese painter Giuseppe Arcimboldo, in paintings that included a famous image of a librarian composed of books (shown on the cover of this essay), as well as portraits of a cook and a butler constructed from the implements of their professions.[26]

Sometimes the humorous effect comes from the way in which play is represented, as in the case of the almost ubiquitous *putti*, cherubs who were represented both with and without wings. Present in ancient Roman art, sculptures of *putti* were revived by Donatello, followed by Agostino di Ducci in what is now known as the 'Chapel of Infants' Games' (*Cappella dei giuochi infantili*) in the cathedral in Rimini. The best-known recruits to this army of *putti* are surely the pair portrayed by Raphael in his *Sistine Madonna* and now ubiquitous on T-shirts for tourists. It has been argued that art historians have 'failed to explain' the expressions of this pair, which are sometimes taken to be serious, sometimes 'impish', and also that they 'function as expressive foils to the Christ Child', since they are unable to see what he sees.[27]

Whatever is the case in Raphael's painting, *putti* are frequently represented as playing and getting into mischief. They dance, stand on their hands, fight one another and drink too much. The peeing *putto* is a recurrent motif, from the fountain in the fifteenth-century romance *Polifilo* to the statue of the *Manneken Pis* in Brussels, the original of which dates from 1618. The

---

[26] Thomas DaCosta Kaufmann, *Arcimboldo: Visual Jokes, Natural History and Still-Life Painting* (Chicago, IL, 2010), 91–114; on the librarian, 96.

[27] Patricia Emison, 'Raphael's Dresden Cherubs', *Zeitschrift für Kunstgeschichte* 65 (2002), 242–50. For a survey of *putti*, see Charles Dempsey, *Inventing the Renaissance Putto* (Chapel Hill, NC, 2001).

playfulness of the *putti* may be interpreted as subversion, and their imitations of adult behaviour as mockery. At the very least, miniaturization encourages distanciation, making the familiar strange thanks to what we might call a 'Lilliput effect'.

Sometimes the artist plays with the spectator, deliberately producing an effect of surprise, if not shock. Surprise (*maraviglia*) is the aim of a number of *trompe l'oeil* paintings from the Italian Renaissance: the fly on the painted ledge tempting the spectator to brush it off or the painted windows from which painted figures eye visitors. A striking example, painted to shock, is the work of Raphael's former pupil Giulio Romano at the Palazzo del Te in Mantua. In the Hall of the Giants (*Sala dei Giganti*), he painted a fresco of a great battle, in which, as the artist-biographer Giorgio Vasari remarked in his life of the painter, the spectator, seeing 'the mountains and buildings falling, cannot but fear that everything is going to collapse in ruins upon him'. Characteristically, Giulio Romano took the *topos* of the naughty *putti* further than usual and represented some of them peeing down onto the viewers of his painted ceiling. Giulio was also an architect and he could not resist an architectural joke, again at the Palazzo del Te, designing a frieze in which some of the usual classical elements, the triglyphs, are displaced, suggesting to the viewer that they are about to fall out.[28]

In the famous 'Sacred Wood' (*Sacro Bosco*), the garden laid out for the Roman nobleman Vicino Orsini at Bomarzo, near Viterbo (discussed at greater length

---

[28] Ernst H. Gombrich, 'Architecture and Rhetoric in Giulio Romano's Palazzo del Te', in *New Light on Old Masters* (Oxford, 1986), 161–70.

in Chapter 5), visitors encountered huge sculptures of monsters, which were probably seen as both alarming and delightful. This suggestion is confirmed by the suggestion in a contemporary discussion of grottoes that they should be furnished with 'frightful or ridiculous masks'. As we have seen, discussions of humour by Castiglione and others suggested that physical deformity – monstrosity – offered an occasion for laughter.[29] The monsters of Bomarzo simply exaggerated a common feature of Renaissance gardens, which often included grottoes that were a scene for 'grotesques', defined by Vasari as 'ridiculous and licentious' images, expressions of 'whims' (*ghiribizzi*).

Carrying surprises a stage further than Bomarzo, some of the fountains in Italian gardens of this period were designed as traps for unwary visitors. The gardens included Caprarola, designed for the Farnese family, and Pratolino, laid out for the Grand Duke Francesco of Tuscany by the artist-engineer Bernardo Buontalenti (who was also the designer of the grotto in the Boboli Gardens in Florence). Approaching the fountains when they were turned off in order to view the sculptures at close quarters, the visitors might be suddenly converted from spectators into victims of a practical joke.[30] Montaigne, who visited Pratolino in 1580, wrote in his journal that he was sitting in the grotto when the seats spouted water, and when he fled the scene, the

---

[29] Horst Bredekamp, *Vicino Orsini und der heilige Wald von Bomarzo* (Worms, 1985); Claudia Lazzaro, *The Italian Renaissance Garden* (New Haven, CT, 1990), 137, 142, 306.

[30] Detlev Heikamp, 'Les merveilles de Pratolino', *L'Oeuil* 171 (1969), 16–27; Luigi Zangheri, *Pratolino: il giardino delle maraviglie* (Florence, 1979).

stairs up to the villa drenched him yet again.[31] Such *scherzi d'acqua*, as they were known at the time, were a sophisticated version of the common Italian practice of throwing water at revellers during Carnival.

Humour in Action

The fountains described above bring us to what might be called 'humour in action', in comedies and in practical jokes. All plays are playful in the sense that they imitate life, like children at play. In Italian, the word *commedia* means both 'play' and 'comedy'. Renaissance Italy was the scene of a lively tradition of religious plays (*sacre rappresentazioni*), as well as presenting a revival of classical tragedy inspired by the plays of Seneca the Younger. Famous examples of this revival include Giangiorgio Trissino's *Sofonisba* (1524) and Giambattista Giraldi Cinthio's *Orbecche* (1541).

Leaving these aside, what follows will concentrate on dramatic performances that were intended to provoke laughter. There was more than one genre of these performances. In Renaissance Italy, the revived classical comedy coexisted with the medieval tradition of the 'farce' (*farsa*). The *commedia dell'arte*, a new cultural form that emerged in the middle of the sixteenth century, may be viewed, like so many new cultural forms, as a hybridization of earlier practices. It combined elements from both comedy and farce, as well as drawing on both the acrobatic and the verbal skills of buffoons and the

---

[31] Michel de Montaigne, *Journal de voyage* (ed. François Rigolot, Paris, 1992), 79. On *scherzi d'acqua*, Lazzaro, *Italian Renaissance Garden*, 65–6.

charlatans (*ciarlatani*) who sold dubious medicines from a stage in the piazza and praised the virtues of their products in speeches that were half-way between classical hyperbole and modern advertising 'hype'. The strength of the *commedia dell'arte*, as Robert Henke has remarked, 'lay in its omnivorous capacity to absorb widely diverse forms, practices, and cultural strains'.[32] In the eighteenth century, Carlo Goldoni was still drawing on this tradition, especially in his early plays, though he abandoned stereotyped masks to create individual characters.[33]

Farces were a 'mixture' (as their name originally implied, especially in the context of cuisine). Among their ingredients were jokes, stage 'business' and acrobatics. Farces in dialect were produced in both the north and the south of the Italian peninsula at this time. In the north, the leading author was the Piedmontese nobleman Giangiorgio Alione, whose plays, including the 'Farce of John the Shoemaker' (*Farsa de Zohan zavatin*), followed a French model. His opposite number in the south was the Neapolitan actor Pietro Antonio Caracciolo. His plays, including 'The Sick Man' and 'The Doctor', were acted at court.

Much better known, at least today, is the so-called 'humanist comedy' or *commedia erudita*. Among the manuscripts of ancient Roman writers discovered by humanists were plays by Plautus. Petrarch, for instance, owned manuscripts of eight of his comedies. Texts by Plautus were performed in Rome in 1468, in Florence

---

[32] Robert Henke, *Performance and Literature in the Commedia dell'Arte* (Cambridge, 2002), 1, and on the *buffoni*, 50–68. On the tradition of the *ciarlatani*, Roberto Tessari, *La Commedia dell'arte* (Rome, 2013), 12–14, 29.
[33] Olga Marchini, *Goldoni e la commedia dell'arte* (Naples, 1912).

in 1476, and in Ferrara in 1486 and on later occasions, such as the wedding of Lucrezia Borgia in 1502. When the humanists began writing their own plays in Italian, they borrowed both plots and characters from Plautus, suitably adapted to fit into the culture of sixteenth-century Italy. Two of the most famous Renaissance comedies, Ariosto's *Suppositi* (1509) and Bibbiena's *Calandria* (1513), adapt the *Menaechmi* of Plautus, as Shakespeare would do in his *Comedy of Errors*. All three plays centre on the adventures of twins, each of whom is regularly mistaken for the other.

On the edge between humanist and popular traditions was Angelo Beolco, nicknamed 'Ruzzante' ('the joker'), who was active as a playwright and an actor, as well as combining the roles of what we call a 'director' and a 'producer'. As a former estate manager, Beolco was well acquainted with the life of peasants, but he also frequented a humanist circle in Padua. His plays about peasants, composed in Paduan dialect, drew on both traditions, farce and humanist comedy, and added something important of his own, presenting peasants as tragic as well as comic figures.[34]

Pietro Aretino, the author of two famous comedies, 'The Master of the Horse' (*Il Marescalco*) and 'The Courtesan' (*La Cortegiana*), both published in 1534, also drew on both traditions, but added a third element to the mix: satire. Notorious for his literary bite, Aretino was described as 'a bad enemy' (*mal nemico*) and as the 'secretary' of Pasquino, a mutilated statue still to be seen

---

[34] Giorgio Padoan, *La commedia rinascimentale veneta (1433–1565)* (Vicenza, 1982); Linda L. Carroll, *Angelo Beolco (il Ruzante)* (Boston, MA, 1990).

Figure 3 Pasquino by Beatrizet
Source: Gift of Mrs. Olga Sichel and Max Philippson, 1962/ Wikimedia Commons

in Rome (on Piazza Pasquino, just off Piazza Navona) who became a kind of mask or spokesperson for anonymous satires on the city's ecclesiastical regime.

A new type of comedy appeared on the scene in

Laughter

sixteenth-century Italy, the *commedia dell'arte* (a name it was given in the eighteenth century). This genre drew once again on both learned and popular traditions, taking characters from Plautus, situations from the farce, and a style of acting from famous clowns such as Domenigo Taiacalze and Zuan Polo Liompardi, both of whom flourished in the early sixteenth century. The *commedia* offered a combination of stereotyped characters, dances, acrobatics and a relative freedom from a fixed script. Improvisation – or, more exactly, semi-improvisation – was the name of the game, assisted, as improvisation often is, by recurrent themes and verbal formulae.[35] Non-verbal communication was particularly important in this genre: the gestures, the acrobatics, the beatings, and the stereotyped stage business (known as *lazzi*). This non-verbal element helps to explain the success of the *commedia* abroad, among audiences who were unlikely to understand what the characters were saying.[36]

All the same, the foreign audiences missed a great deal, given the importance of language in Italian comedy – a kind of 'verbal acrobatics' or 'vocal virtuosity'.[37] The repertoire included jokes, slang, alliteration, parody, nonsense, rapid changes of mood and a mixture of languages and dialects. The Venetian actor Andrea Calmo, for instance, used different dialects to comic effect in his *Spagnola*s (1549), in which one soldier

---

[35] Albert Lord, *The Singer of Tales* (Cambridge, MA, 1960); Tim Fitzpatrick, *The Relation between Oral and Literate Performance Processes in the Commedia dell'Arte* (Lewiston, ID, 1995).
[36] Kathleen M. Lea, *Italian Popular Comedy* (Oxford, 1934); Henke, *Performance and Literature*.
[37] Henke, *Performance and Literature*, 19, 63.

speaks Bergamasque and another a mixture of Italian and Greek, while other characters speak Venetian. In the *commedia dell'arte*, which drew on comic classics such as Calmo's letters (and, later, on the *Bertoldo* of Giulio Cesare Croce), this kind of mixture became standardized. Each of the stereotyped characters was associated with a specific dialect and specific verbal formulae, as well as with a specific mask. Capitano, the boastful soldier (a character borrowed from Plautus) made his exaggerated claims in Neapolitan with a dash of Spanish. Pantalone, the old man (Shakespeare's lean, slippered and spectacled 'Pantaloon'), spoke Venetian. So did the cunning or simple servant Zanni (Venetian for 'Giovanni'). In mock-homage to the two most famous Italian universities, Paduan or Bolognese was spoken by Dottore or Graziano, a professor who claimed to demonstrate what everyone already knows, such as 'a man who walks is not dead'. The leading actress Isabella Andreini created Babel on the stage when she pretended to go mad and to parody the roles of her colleagues, using all their dialects.[38]

Central to the plot of many comedies was some kind of deceit (*inganno*), as in the case of Machiavelli's *Mandragola* (1526). It was sometimes emphasized in the title, from *Gl'ingannati* (1531) written and performed by the Academy of the *Intronati*, to a whole series of plays from the seventeenth and eighteenth centuries. Deceit was also central to the *beffa* – in other words, the practical joke, an important element in Italian culture in the fifteenth and sixteenth centuries, and one involving some leading figures of the Renaissance, including

---

[38] Tessari, *La Commedia dell'arte*.

Laughter

Machiavelli and the Florentine architect Filippo Brunelleschi. The point of the *beffa* was to deceive the victim in a manner that was usually humiliating. As in the case of witticisms, surprise was a key element in success.

Practical jokes may be found in many – if not in all – cultures, but they seem to have had unusual appeal in Italy at this time. To look at the references to such jokes worldwide in the famous *Motif-Index of Folk-Literature* compiled by the American folklorist Stith Thompson is to be impressed by the number of Italian Renaissance examples, especially in Florence, 'la capitale de la *beffa*'.[39] If we examine a similar index, this time to motifs recurrent in the Italian short story of the Renaissance, the *novella*, the list is even more impressive, amounting to an unusual emphasis on this form of humour in Italy. For category X 0-99, 'Humor of Discomfiture', for instance, Thompson gives four examples, but the Italian collection gives twenty. In the case of category K 1200-99, 'Deception into a Humiliating Position', Thompson gives twenty-seven examples (including eight from Boccaccio), while the Italian collection offers no fewer than seventy-two. Italians, especially Tuscans, appear to have been obsessed by this theme.[40] Why was this the case? A possible answer to this question is that the *beffa* was an appropriate form

---

[39] André Rochon (ed.) *Formes et significations de la beffa*, 2 vols. (Paris, 1972–5), vol. I, 28. The discussion that follows repeats some points that I made in Peter Burke, 'Frontiers of the Comic in Early Modern Italy', in Jan Bremmer and Herman Roodenburg (eds.) *A Cultural History of Humour* (Cambridge, 1997), 61–75.

[40] Stith Thompson, *Motif-Index of Folk-Literature* (1932–6: revised edn, 6 vols., Bloomington, IN, 1956–8); Dominic P. Rotunda, *Motif-Index of the Italian Novella* (Bloomington, IN, 1942).

of joking in a competitive culture which was also what might be called a 'culture of trickery', rather than a 'culture of force': in other words – the words of Machiavelli – a land of 'foxes' rather than 'lions'. Boccaccio's *Decameron* makes an obvious starting-point for the study of the genre. The tricks occur in 27 stories altogether, and the terms *beffa*, *beffare* and *beffatore* are used eighty times.[41] Later in the century, *beffe* recur in the stories of another Florentine, Francesco Sacchetti. In the fifteenth century, they are to be found in two more storytellers, one from Salerno and the other from Bologna: Masuccio Salernitano and Giovanni Sabadino degli Arienti.[42] *Beffe* are still more frequent in sixteenth-century texts. In the stories of Antonfrancesco Grazzini (died 1584), 'the *beffa* is the key', as a French critic puts it, occurring in 18 stories.[43] They are even more important in the Lombard writer Matteo Bandello: seventy *beffe* in 214 *novelle*.

Poems and plays reinforce the importance of the *beffa* in Renaissance Italy. To return to Folengo's mock-epic *Baldus*, one of its most important characters is the trickster Cingar, a friend of the protagonist. His most memorable trick (borrowed by François Rabelais on behalf of his character Panurge) occurs when he is travelling by ship along with a flock of sheep and, quarrelling with their owner, throws one animal overboard, who is instantly followed by all the others.

---

[41] Alfredo Barbina (ed.) *Concordanze del 'Decameron'* (Florence, 1969); cf. Giuseppe Mazzotti, *The World at Play in Boccaccio's Decameron* (Princeton, NJ, 1986).
[42] Rochon (ed.) *Formes*.
[43] Rochon (ed.) *Formes*, vol. I, 45–98. Cf. Robert J. Rodini, *A. F. Grazzini* (Madison, WI, 1970), 153–6.

Laughter

The *beffa* was regarded as a work of art. It was sometimes described as 'beautiful' (*bella*). Practical jokes form an essential part of the plot of some Renaissance comedies, such as Pietro Aretino's *Il Marescalco* (1534), a Carnival entertainment at the court of the Duke of Mantua in which the Master of the Horse is informed that the Duke wishes him to marry. Bad news for him, since his tastes are not for the opposite sex, but he goes through the ceremony, only to discover that his 'bride' is a page. The incident is described in the play as a *burla* (Act 5, Scene 11), a term often applied to a gentle version of the *beffa*. Tricks of this kind occur in some of the classical dramas imitated by the playwrights of the Renaissance – in Terence's *Adelphi*, for instance. In the case of *Il Marescalco*, the Master of the Horse does not seem to be the only victim of Aretino's wit. When he was safe in Venice, Aretino revised his comedy to allude to the Duke of Mantua's own failure to marry as expected.[44]

The most famous example of the *beffa* in the Renaissance, however, is surely the fifteenth-century story of a trick played on a fat carpenter, nicknamed *il grasso legnaiolo*, by none other than Filippo Brunelleschi. This example is all the more interesting because it plays with the idea of identity in a period that Burckhardt famously described as an age of individualism. The victim, Manetto, a member of a festive *brigata* that included

---

[44] Paul Larivaille, *Pietro Aretino* (1980: Italian translation, Rome, 1997), 178–85; Deanna Shemek, 'Aretino's *Marescalco*', *Renaissance Studies* 16 (2002), 366–80. Cf. Burke, 'Frontiers of the Comic'; M. Chiabò and Federico Doglio (eds.) *Satira e beffe nelle commedie europee del Rinascimento* (Rome, 2002). Della Casa mentions the *beffa* enacted in the *Adelphi* in ch. 19 of the *Galateo*.

Brunelleschi and the sculptor Donatello, failed to turn up to a Sunday supper. The group felt snubbed (*scornati*) and planned revenge, conspiring to persuade the carpenter that he was not himself but a local good-for-nothing named Matteo Mannini. The jokers all addressed the carpenter as 'Matteo', persuaded others to do so and put on such a convincing collective performance that he became confused and even began to believe that they were right.[45]

These stories raise the question: was the *beffa* simply a literary game, or was it a social custom at this time? Some archives provide an answer. Practical jokes are known to have been played in a few courts in Renaissance Italy. At the court of Milan in 1492, for instance, Princess Beatrice d'Este played a trick on the ambassador of Ferrara, causing his garden to be invaded by wild animals which killed his chickens, to the great amusement of Beatrice's husband, Lodovico Sforza, the ruler of the state.[46] Other evidence comes from judicial records regarding jokes that gave offence and so led to proceedings in court.[47]

Calling in the law reveals the limits of joking, the frontier between relatively harmless deception and more serious trickery.[48] In northern Italy in the sixteenth century, *dare la burla* was a standard phrase employed

---

[45] For the text, see https://archive.org/details/ita-bnc-in2-00002206-001. Cf. Lauro Martines, 'The Tale as Historical Testimony' (1995: repr. in *Strong Words: Writing and Social Strain in the Italian Renaissance* (Baltimore, MD, 2001), 167–81, at 178–80.

[46] Francesco Malaguzzi Valeri, *La corte di Lodovico il Moro*, 4 vols. (Milan, 1913–23), vol. I, 560–1.

[47] Gherardo Ortalli, 'Il giudice e la taverna', in Ortalli (ed.) *Gioco e giustizia nell'Italia di Comune* (Treviso and Rome, 1993), 49–70.

[48] Gherardo Ortalli, 'Uncertain Thresholds of Tolerance: Games and Crisis in the Middle Ages', *Ludica* 1 (1995), 56–68.

to describe false promises of marriage.[49] Again, in an age when jokes were often insulting and insults sometimes took playful forms, it was inevitable that someone would overstep the customary limits and that some cases would end up in court. The difficulty of defining the frontier between the comic and the serious is apparent in these records. The threshold was sometimes barely visible but extremely dangerous to cross, depending on the definition of the situation by the victim, his (usually his) social status and his sensitivity. Mannino, for instance, was so embarrassed by the trick played on him that he left Florence for good. His story reminds us that in a culture where the values of honour and shame were central, this kind of joke was not a joke, at least from the victim's point of view.

Sometimes the court took the victim's complaint seriously, sometimes not. In sixteenth-century Bologna, for instance, one victim of a verbal assault (by means of a sonnet) complained to a tribunal, but the judges considered that the text was not defamatory. It was only 'a joke, containing something laughable'.[50] On the other hand, the painter Michelangelo da Caravaggio, who had a gift for getting himself into trouble, was called before the Tribunal of the Governor of Rome in 1603 in company with other painters, charged with what their colleague Giovanni Baglioni called 'verses in my dishonour'. Caravaggio was found guilty and sent to prison.[51]

---

[49] Edward Muir and Guido Ruggiero (eds.) *Sex and Gender* (Baltimore, MD, 1990), 351.
[50] Claudia Evangelisti, 'Libelli famosi', *Annali della Fondazione Einaudi* 26 (1992), 181–227, at 221.
[51] The verses can be found at https://arthistoryproject.com/artists/caravaggio/poems-in-mockery-of-....

Aggression: The Dark Side of Laughter

Enough has been said to suggest that play was not always harmless and that jokes were not perceived as amusing by everyone. Burckhardt was well aware of this, when he presented the *beffa* (or the *burla*, as he preferred to call it) as offering 'heartless and pointless malice', along with humour.[52] These points bear further development. Indeed, they require it for the better understanding of Italian culture at this time.

Play in the Renaissance had its dark side. Today, it may come as something of a shock to discover quite how aggressive were the favourite forms of what we call 'leisure' or 'relaxation'. Play was often violent, and violence was sometimes playful, a point that Mikhail Bakhtin emphasized in the case of sixteenth-century France, placing what he called the 'joyful thrashings' described by Rabelais in a general history of laughter.[53] In Italy, examples of playful violence included charivaris and protests. Charivaris, known as *scampanate*, were responses by the young men of a village or an urban parish to the marriage of one of 'their' women to an older man or to an outsider. They took the form of what the English called 'rough music' – in other words, keeping the newly married couple awake with their noise until they were bought off with drink.[54]

Protests, however serious, were also a form of theatre.

---

[52] Jacob Burckhardt, *Civilization of the Renaissance in Italy* (1860: English translation, London, 1944), 95.
[53] Bakhtin, *Rabelais and his World* (1965: English translation, Cambridge, MA, 1968), 196–209. The thrashings mainly occur in the fourth book of *Gargantua and Pantagruel*.
[54] Carlo Ginzburg, 'Charivari', *Quaderni Storici* 17 (1982), 164–77.

Violence was ritualized, while riots sometimes took a festive form. In Friuli, for instance, in the north-east of Italy, vendettas and conflicts between factions often took place during festivals such as Carnival and on one occasion the winners displayed the bodies of their enemies as if they were 'hunting trophies'.[55] In the famous revolt of Naples in 1647 against the tax on fruit, an official was lynched and his head covered with pieces of melon rind and orange peel in the style of a portrait by Arcimboldo, at once an insult to the corpse and a reminder of the tax that sparked the revolt. Some gestures of revolt were recurrent, such as looting the houses of members of the upper class. They included the so-called 'ritual sackings' of houses in the interval between the death of a pope and the election of his successor – a power vacuum, and so a time, like Carnival, when anything was permitted (so it was thought).[56]

Nineteenth-century writers on the Renaissance, whether poets or historians, were not amused. They were both horrified and fascinated by what they saw as the extreme violence of the period. Think of the poisonings attributed to the Borgia family; of Alfred de Musset's drama *Lorenzaccio* (1834), in which the protagonist assassinates his cousin the Duke of Florence; or of Robert Browning's dramatic poem *My Last Duchess* (1842), in which a duke has his wife killed to avenge her apparent infidelity. Jacob Burckhardt's essay on the Renaissance (1860) shows traces of this fascination with assassination and vendetta, to which he devotes nearly three pages

---

[55] Edward Muir, *Mad Blood Stirring: Vendetta and Factions in Friuli during the Renaissance* (Baltimore, MD, 1993).
[56] Ginzburg, 'Saccheggi rituali', *Quaderni Storici* 65 (1987), 615–36.

of his chapter on 'Morality and Religion'. In similar fashion, Johan Huizinga, in his *Autumn of the Middle Ages* (1919), described the fourteenth and fifteen centuries as an age that smelled of 'blood and roses', combining the love of beauty with a propensity for violence.[57]

It was certainly an age of rough play. The martial games loved by the upper classes might inflict serious injuries. Duke Federico of Urbino lost an eye in a joust, a loss that is skilfully hidden in his most famous portrait, by Piero della Francesca – in profile. Only in the sixteenth century did less violent games such as football and tennis gradually replace jousts and tournaments. At a popular level, the *battagliola* claimed casualties when mock-battles turned real and knives were drawn. In Siena in 1318, the usual stone-throwing game on the Campo went wrong, leading to ten deaths and many injuries. In Florence in 1387, injuries and arrests followed the traditional battle at the bridge of Santa Trinita.[58] In the 'stick wars' in Venice, despite the wearing of various types of defensive armour, 'almost every year a few unfortunates were killed', while injuries were common. In Caravia's celebration of one of these encounters, the two champions both meet their deaths.[59]

Conflict was an essential part of the *commedia dell'arte*, including both verbal duels and physical ones.[60] One recurrent scene featured Pantalone pulling out Zanni's teeth, while beatings were as frequent as in

---

[57] J. B. Bullen, *The Myth of the Renaissance in Nineteenth-Century Writing* (Oxford, 1994).
[58] Alessandra Rizzi, *Ludus/ludere: giocare in Italia alla fine del medio evo* (Rome, 1995), 43–4.
[59] Davis, *The War of the Fists*, 78, 100.
[60] Henke, *Performance and Literature*, 13, 23, 26–7, 36–7.

Laughter

the later puppet show of Punch and Judy. The 'slapstick' humour literally involved slapping or being slapped with a stick. Descriptions of practical jokes in the short stories (*novelle*) that were so popular at this time sometimes involve physical violence. In two of these stories, one by Antonfrancesco Grazzini of Florence and the other by Matteo Bandello of Milan, what is supposed to be funny is the castration of the victim.[61] Actual cases of violence were sometimes celebrated in verse, as in the notorious example of the Venetian Lorenzo Venier, who described the gang rape of the courtesan Anzola Zaffetta in a poem entitled *Il Trentuno della Zaffetta* (1532).

In prose, Machiavelli described how Cesare Borgia took revenge on some of the soldiers in his service, whom he suspected of treason, tricking them into entering his lodgings in Sinigaglia (now Senigallia) without their weapons and having them strangled there. Machiavelli's cool description of the event resembles the narrative of a *beffa*, despite its fatal consequences. Cesare is described as 'a great pretender' (*grandissimo simulatore*), whose deception of his enemies revealed his cunning and wisdom (*astuzie e sagacità*).[62]

Carnival (discussed in more detail in Chapter 5) was not only a time of joy but also a time of violence – indeed, of joyous violence. According to the statutes of a society

---

[61] Antonfrancesco Grazzini, *Le Cene* (1549), book 1, no. 2; Matteo Bandello, *Novelle* (1554), book 2, no. 20. Cf. Barbara Viscardi Balduzzi, 'Dalla *beffa* al *caso*: la novella del prete castrato', in Ugo Rozzo (ed.) *Matteo Bandello* (Tortona, 1982), 223–31.

[62] Niccolò Machiavelli, *Descrizione del modo tenuto dal Duca Valentino nello ammazzare Vitellozzo Vitelli, Oliverotto da Fermo, il Signor Pagolo e il duca di Gravina Orsini* (1503), in his *Opere*, ed. Mario Bonfantini (Milan and Naples, 1954), 457–64.

in Siena called, appropriately enough, the 'Rough Ones' (*Rozzi*), games were compulsory for members during Carnival, and 'no one' (on pain of a fine) 'can avoid allowing themselves' to be drenched, knocked down or have wine thrown in their faces.[63] There was worse to come. In the eighteenth and nineteenth centuries, the Venetian Carnival would be celebrated as an exemplar of civilized behaviour, but in the late sixteenth century it was not uncommon for participants to be killed, whether by accident, in a spontaneous brawl or to settle old scores.

Physical violence was accompanied by visual, verbal and what we might call 'psychological violence'. Public insults might be regarded as a kind of foreplay, a provocation to violence, as in the case of a written insult (*cartello infamante*) attached to the door of an embroiderer in Rome in 1620, including the challenge, 'challenge me, you cuckold' (*dami la querela, beccone*). Not for nothing were these insults known as 'pasquinades', the private equivalent of the satires pasted to the famous statue, satires that formed an important part of the early modern Roman public sphere.[64]

The sonnets of the Italian Renaissance included not only love poems but also what might be called 'hate poems', designed to give the victim a 'short sharp shock' and also to destroy him or her socially, thus offering examples of what Mikhail Bakhtin called 'uncrowning'. Lorenzo Venier's attack on Anzola Zaffetta is one such

---

[63] Quoted in Laura Riccò, *Giuoco e teatro nelle veglie di Siena* (Rome, 1993), 40–1.

[64] On Pasquin, Larivaille, *Pietro Aretino*, 57–64. On private pasquinades, Peter Burke, 'Insult and Blasphemy in Early Modern Italy', in *Historical Anthropology of Early Modern Italy* (Cambridge, 1987), 95–109.

case. Another member of the Venier family, Maffio, attacked another Venetian courtesan, Veronica Franco, in a similar way (Veronica, herself a poet, gave as good as she got).[65] Aretino, who might be said to have had an elective affinity with Pasquino and wrote some of his most biting verses in his name, was a master of this form of joyous violence, striking the victim like a dagger. In fact, one response to his sonnets was a real dagger: Aretino was wounded in a failed attempt to kill him in 1525.[66] Conversely, the poet Niccolò Franco, who quarrelled with Aretino, his former employer, and wrote no fewer than 297 sonnets against him, was knifed by a follower of his victim. The comic poet Francesco Berni also attacked Aretino, but only in verse.

Verses of this kind might be described as a form of psychological violence. Italians called it *scherno*, meaning 'scorn'. The *Galateo* condemned *scherni*, distinguishing them from the *beffa*, a trick played 'for fun' (*per solazzo*). Della Casa admitted that tricks were often taken badly, 'turning from a joke into a brawl' (*di scherzo fanno zuffa*) since no one liked to be deceived. For this reason, he recommended jokes that were 'friendly' and 'gentle' (*dolce*).[67] The recommendation was somewhat unrealistic. The whole point of a *beffa*, to judge by contemporary accounts of it, was precisely to humiliate the victim. Literary descriptions of the *beffa* sometimes describe it as a form of shaming. In the titles of the stories by the Bolognese

---

[65] Longhi, *Lusus*, 7; cf. Margaret F. Rosenthal, *The Honest Courtesan: Veronica Franco* (Chicago, IL, 1992), and Dolora C. Wojciehowski, 'Veronica Franco vs. Maffio Venier', *Italica* 83 (2006), 367–90.
[66] Details in Larivaille, *Pietro Aretino*, 115–19.
[67] Della Casa, *Il Galateo*, ch. 19.

writer Sabadino degli Arienti, for instance, four of the victims are described as 'shamed' (*vergognato*).[68] The word reminds us that honour and shame were among the central values of Renaissance Italy, as visible in play as in the serious world of work. A recurrent theme in both life and art was revenge (*vendetta*). Burckhardt's examples of bloody revenge in the everyday life of the upper classes at this time have parallels in the domain of laughter. In the *Book of the Courtier*, even the gentle Lady Emilia refers to playful revenge. Connoisseurs of the practical joke appreciated examples of retaliation (*contracambio*) – in other words, the theme of the biter bit: *il beffatore beffato*.[69]

Were people more aggressive in this period than we are today? To this obvious question, all that historians can truthfully answer is that they do not know. Where historians can make a specific contribution to the study of violence concerns what might be called its 'morphology' – in other words, the particular forms that it has taken in different cultures or social groups. Since nobles wore swords at their sides, while many other adult males carried knives, the transition between playful and serious aggression in Renaissance Italy was often extremely swift. Certain forms of play, notably gambling on the fall of dice, were particularly prone to erupt in this way. As preachers often pointed out, gambling was an occasion of violence. Beyond this, one can only speculate. It is tempting to say that in Renaissance Italy, there was a relative preference for

[68] Giovanni Sabadino degli Arienti, *Novelle Porretane* (1483), nos. 1, 16, 31, 35.
[69] Burckhardt, *Renaissance*, 265–7; Castiglione, *Il Cortegiano*, book 2, ch. 53; Bandello, *Novelle*, book 1, no. 3.

Laughter

deceit over open aggression, but the popularity of playful – and not-so-playful – physical violence must not be forgotten.

4
Play:
For and Against

Like other parts of Europe, such as Britain, France and Spain, Italy was the scene of a major debate about play in the early modern period, in which theologians, moralists, physicians, town councillors and humanists discussed the dangers, and to a lesser extent the benefits, of different forms of play. This debate will be presented so far as possible in the words of the participants, as if in a courtroom where the case for the prosecution is followed by the case for the defence.

Criticizing Play

Play, or at least many forms of it, had often been criticized in medieval Italy. Moderate criticisms came from the urban authorities, concerned with violent games because they were a threat to public order, and with gambling because it impoverished many players and often led to violence. More extreme criticisms of play – as diabolical, for instance – were sometimes heard from the clergy, especially the friars, though some of them offered the milder argument that play offered occasions of sin. During the Renaissance, these criticisms were repeated and extended, while some new arguments were put forward. Among the humanists, Petrarch the individualist presented his own case against play. He dismissed physical games for emphasizing the body at the expense of the mind, and criticized tournaments not only as dangerous, but as 'childish' as well.[1] In the dialogue on the family written by Leonbattista Alberti, one of the characters criticizes jousting as dangerous, useless, expensive and likely to generate 'more envy than friendship, more blame than praise' (*piú invidia che amistà, piú biasimo che lodo*).[2] In the sixteenth century, Sperone Speroni, a former student of Pietro Pomponazzi, who once described philosophy as a game, was proud to say that he used his *ozio* (his leisure from teaching at the University of Padua) not to participate in feasts and balls, or to play cards or dice (*non feste o balli, non carte o dadi*), but to write his dialogues.[3] As a group, the humanists were ambivalent about dancing, some of them emphasizing the traditional moral critique while others, such as

---

[1] Francesco Petrarca, *De remediis* and *Seniles,* quoted in Alessandra Rizzi, *Ludus/ludere: giocare in Italia alla fine del medio evo* (Rome, 1995), 40.
[2] Leonbattisti Alberti, *I libri della famiglia*, ed. Ruggiero Romano and Alberto Tenenti (Turin, 1969), 194. Cf. Tiziana Tibo, 'Il gioco nelle parole dei predicatori, dei maestri, dei legislatori italiani del '400 e '500', in Paolo Procaccioli (ed.) *Studi per le 'Sorti'* (Treviso, 2007), 191–206.
[3] Sperone Speroni, *Dialoghi* (Venice, 1596), repr. in Mario Pozzi (ed.) *Trattatisti del '500* (Milan and Naples, 1978), 683–94, at 692. Cf. Andreas Hermann Fischer, *Spielen und Philosophieren zwischen Spätmittelalter und Früher Neuzeit* (Göttingen, 2016), 13 (on Pomponazzi) and 146–55 (on Speroni).

Jean-Jacques Rousseau later, viewed the dance as a form of education.[4] More common was the re-iteration or elaboration of traditional criticisms. The city authorities continued to forbid or limit certain forms of play on three main grounds. The first was that these forms were dangerous, not only in the obvious case of mock-battles, where the participants ran the risk of serious injuries or even death, but also that of gambling, which might reduce an unfortunate player to poverty. The second reason was that these forms of play were occasions of public disorder. In the third place, some kinds of play were considered to be indecorous, and so a threat to the honour of the commune. In early sixteenth-century Venice, for instance, a traditional Carnival dance, the *tripudio*, was abolished on these grounds. The diarist Marin Sanudo shared this view, criticizing the activities of revellers in the Carnivals of 1529 and 1533, in the first case imitating a flagellant, 'something that was not to be tolerated' (*cosa che non era da soportar*), and, in the second case, walking in procession with pipers and trumpeters like the Doge, 'which in my opinion was not well done' (*che per mia oppinion non fo ben fatto*).[5] On occasion, a municipality might take action on religious grounds. In 1630, when the plague returned to Florence, a chronicler wrote that 'All gambling dens were prohibited as well as all meetings ... especially where they played ball games ... in order not just to avoid crowds of people but also the moral causes of contagion that are sins'.

[4] Alessandro Arcangeli, *Davide o Salomè? Il dibattito europeo sulla danza nella prima età moderna* (Rome, 2000), 108–14.
[5] Marin Sanudo, *I diarii*, 58 vols. (Venice, 1879–1903), vol. XLIX, 422, and vol. LVII, 548.

Play: For and Against

At this time, some physicians, following the humanist Girolamo Fracastoro, believed that plague was spread via invisibly small living particles, not unlike the 'droplets' of coronavirus.[6]

As for the clergy, the friars, notably the Franciscans Bernardino da Siena and Roberto da Lecce and the Dominicans Giovanni Dominici and Girolamo Savonarola, were the leaders of a campaign against many forms of play, either because they were immoral in themselves or because they offered occasions of sin.[7] Bernardino condemned mock-battles such as the 'stone wars' in Perugia. Savonarola, who considered it his mission to make Florence a city of God, prevented the usual battle of stones from taking place during the Carnival of 1495. He also rejected poetry on the grounds that such 'lying and childish games' (*giochi mendaci e puerile*) corrupted youth with their 'dirt' (*sporcizia*). He was presumably thinking of love lyrics in the manner of Petrarch.[8]

Games of chance were condemned as occasions of sin because fights were likely to break out, and also because the loser might blaspheme. Bernardino, who regarded betting as a form of theft, was apparently the first to claim that Lucifer was the inventor of gambling, but

---

[6] Francesco Rondinelli, quoted in John Henderson, *Florence under Siege* (New Haven, CT, 2019), 96.

[7] Alessandra Rizzi, 'Chiesa, gioco e società nel Rinascimento', in Francesca Aceto and Francesco Lucioli (eds.) *Giocare tra Medioevo ed età moderna* (Treviso and Rome, 2019), 74–86.

[8] Rizzi, *Ludus*, 144; cf. Lauro Martines, *Fire in the City: Savonarola and the Struggle for the Soul of Renaissance Florence* (Oxford, 2006). Savonarola's critique of poetry is quoted in Gigliola Fragnito, *Rinascimento perduto: la letteratura Italiana sotto gli occhi dei censori (secoli XV–XVII)* (Bologna, 2019), 70.

Dominici was also hostile to the practice.⁹ Dancing was viewed as another occasion of sin, for the obvious sexual reasons. In their condemnations, preachers liked to cite the New Testament story of Salomé, who asked for the head of St John the Baptist as the reward for her dance for King Herod. Dancing in church was regarded as a sin, and the commune of Perugia forbade it following a sermon delivered by Bernardino in 1425. As a substitute for these forms of play, Savonarola encouraged singing hymns (*laude*), some of which were composed by his friend the humanist Girolamo Benivieni.

Bernardino and other friars also urged and organized what have become known as the 'bonfires of the vanities', in which the 'vanities' included musical instruments – accompaniments to the dance – as well as cards and backgammon boards. One of these bonfires took place in Florence in 1424, and another, encouraged by Savonarola, in the same city in 1497, a year before he was himself burned for heresy on Piazza della Signoria.

A concern with decorum was not limited to Sanudo. Gian Maria Giberti, the Bishop of Verona, condemned preachers who 'tell ridiculous stories and old wives' tales in the manner of buffoons' (*more scurrarum*).[10] The Italian humanist Fausto Andrelini was condemned by a German colleague for playing to the gallery by making

---

[9] Rizzi, *Ludus*, 35, 143. Cf. Iris Origo, *The World of San Bernardino* (London, 1963); Franco Mormando, *The Preacher's Demons: Bernardino of Siena and the Social Underground of Early Renaissance Italy* (Chicago, IL, 1999).

[10] Giberti is quoted by Angelo Grazioli, *G. M. Giberti* (Verona, 1955). Cf. Adriano Prosperi, *Tra Evangelismo e Controriforma: G. M. Giberti (1495–1553)* (Rome, 1969).

Play: For and Against

jokes during his lectures.[11] For the upper classes, decorum increasingly meant distinguishing themselves from those below them in the social hierarchy – in particular, the peasants – and so withdrawing from at least some forms of popular culture. The Counter-Reformation campaign against play, which will be discussed in Chapter 6, both revived and extended this earlier critique.

Defending Play

Where the critique of play came from two main groups, the civic authorities and the clergy (especially the friars), the defenders were more dispersed. They included humanists, noblemen, lawyers, physicians, poets and even theologians. For example, a treatise on sin published in 1525 offered a defence of dancing from an unexpected quarter, since its author, Cardinal Tommaso Cajetan, was the head of the order of Dominicans. Cajetan argued that dancing was not a sin in itself, and that it would be rash to forbid peasants (*rustici*) to dance on Sunday since, otherwise, they might become a threat to public order.[12]

In the great debate on play in early modern Europe, in which Italians took part, the arguments for the defence included health, education and the human need for recreation.[13] As one speaker in Alberti's family dialogue

---

[11] '[I]ocis quibusdam magis festivis quam doctis plausum rudium auditorium captans' (Beatus Rhenanus, *Vita Erasmi*, 1536).
[12] Arcangeli, *Davide o Salomè?* 103–4; Arcangeli, 'Dance under Trial: The Moral Debate, 1200–1600', *Dance Research* 12 (1994), 127–55, at 130–1.
[13] Alessandro Arcangeli, *Recreation in the Renaissance: Attitudes Towards Leisure and Pastimes in European Culture, 1350–1700* (Basingstoke, 2003).

remarks, a balanced life should include both *negozio* (including both trade and politics) and *ozio*, a term that ranged from idleness to the leisure that allows study. Play in the form of exercise was regarded, then as now, as good for one's health. 'Exercise helps a great deal', according to a speaker in Alberti's dialogue: *molto giova l'esercizio*. The philosopher-physician Marsilio Ficino agreed. In his book 'On Life' (*De vita*), he argued that scholars are particularly vulnerable to melancholy, but also that melancholy could be corrected by exercise. Ficino also claimed that Pythagoras, Socrates and Plato were all accustomed to 'joke seriously and play assiduously' (*iocari serio et studiosissime ludere*).[14] Other physicians also argued in favour of play as a means of relaxing tension and relieving melancholy. Girolamo Mercuriale, for instance, claimed that ancient dances were a form of exercise that promoted health, although he criticized modern dances because they took place at an inappropriate time, after supper, thus interfering with digestion. The acrobat Arcangelo Turcaro was another writer who suggested that dancing is beneficial because it is gentle and relaxing.[15]

Play was also regarded as a means of education. The private school directed by the fifteenth-century humanist Vittorino da Feltre was supposed to be not only a house of wisdom but also a house of joy (*Casa Zoiosa*). He

---

[14] Quoted by Paula Findlen, 'Jokes of Nature and Jokes of Knowledge', *Renaissance Quarterly* 43 (1990), 292–331, at 294. Cf. Andreas Hermann Fischer, 'Ficinos ernste Spiele mit den Sophisten', in his *Spielen und Philosophieren*, 136–46.

[15] Alessandro Arcangeli, 'Dance and Health', *Dance Research* 18 (2000), 3–30, at 12; Arcangeli, 'Dance under Trial', 142; Arcangeli and Vivian Nutton (eds.) *Girolamo Mercuriale* (Florence, 2007).

included exercise in the curriculum, and for this reason he was recently described as 'the first official P.E. teacher'.[16] Hunting and martial exercises such as jousts and tournaments were commonly regarded as training for war. Even mock-battles such as the Venetian 'stick wars' were officially encouraged, at least in the fourteenth century, for this reason. In the sixteenth century, the Jesuits allowed play in their colleges, including football, tennis, riding at the ring, chess, dancing, and jumping over the horse.[17] The priest Antonio Scaino defended tennis because it kept young people from idleness.[18] In his book on a Christian education, Cardinal Silvio Antoniano advocated *palla*, 'much recommended by doctors', and *trucco* (a kind of croquet). He also allowed what he called 'decent jesting' (*onesto motteggiare*).[19]

In his treatise on games, Innocentio Ringhieri defended them as a means of displaying and transmitting knowledge to adults. In his dialogue on the same subject, Girolamo Bargagli noted that some games required a thorough knowledge of vernacular classics such as the works of Petrarch and Ariosto, while both knowledge and intelligence were required in the game of making and solving *imprese*, the emblems employed as personal devices.

---

[16] William H. Woodward, *Vittorino da Feltre and Other Humanist Educators* (London, 1897); Michele Rossi, *Pedagogia e corte nel Rinascimento* (Venice, 2016), 123–52; Dawn Duran, 'Vittorino da Feltre, the first official P.E. teacher', https://afterthoughtsblog.net/2016/12/first-pe-teacher.html.

[17] Robert C. Davis, *The War of the Fists: Popular Culture and Public Violence in Late Renaissance Venice* (New York, 1994), 15; François de Dainville, *L'éducation des jésuites* (Paris, 1978).

[18] Antonio Scaino, *Trattato del giuocho della palla* (Venice, 1555), quoted in Fischer, *Spielen und Philosophieren*, 222.

[19] Silvio Antoniano, *Tre libri dell'educatione Cristiana dei figliuoli* (Verona, 1584), book 3, chs. 47–9.

The most important justification of all was that play was a response to the human need for recreation. A common metaphor employed at this time was that of the bow, emphasizing the need to loosen the bowstring after shooting – in other words, to relax. It was for this reason that the fourteenth-century Florentine monk Giovanni dalle Celle recognized the need for what he called 'playful and laughable matters' (*cose giochevoli e di riso*). The humanist Giovanni Pontano defended what he called 'relaxing the mind' (*relaxatio animi*). The scholar Piero Vettori referred to stories as a kind of 'medicine'.[20] Girolamo Cardano – who was, among other things, a physician – defended games of chance as a relief from stress, as well as a means of gaining friends and of acquiring knowledge of the character of one's fellow-citizens.[21]

In Castiglione's dialogue on the perfect courtier, Bernardo da Bibbiena, well known in real life for his many jokes, described laughter as an escape from the 'annoying troubles' (*noiose molestie*) of which our life is full. Pietro Aretino also wrote of play as a compensation for the troubles (*fastidi*) of everyday life.[22] In similar fashion, Giovanni Della Casa argued in his *Galateo* that it was impossible for humans to live their hard lives without some 'respite' (*sollazzo*).[23] In two famous

---

[20] Quoted in Fragnito, *Rinascimento perduto*, 12.
[21] Girolamo Cardano, *De ludo aleae* (*c.* 1564: English translation, *The Book on Games of Chance*, New York, 1961), section 4. Cf. Oystein Ore, *Cardano: The Gambling Scholar* (Princeton, NJ, 1953).
[22] Baldassare Castiglione, *Il Cortegiano* (1528: ed. Bruno Maier, Turin, 1964), book 2, ch. 45; Pietro Aretino, *Le carte parlanti* (1550: new edn, Palermo, 1992).
[23] Giovanni Della Casa, *Il Galateo* (1558: ed. Dino Provenzal, Milan, 1950), ch. 19.

Play: For and Against

cases, play is presented as a means of escape or recovery from crisis: escape from the plague in the case of Boccaccio's *Decameron,* and recovery from the siege of Siena (1554–5) in the dialogue on games by Girolamo Bargagli.

Playwrights were well aware that Aristotle had described the function of tragedy as the 'cleansing' (*catharsis*) of the emotions. Poets contributed to the justification of play. Francesco Berni defended his comic verse as a means to 'help restore oneself' (*ricrearsi un poco*), producing 'frivolities' (*bagatelle*) 'to pass the time'. The Florentine painter Angelo Bronzino admitted writing poetry 'to pass the time and refresh my brain' (*per passar tempo e'l cervel ricriarmi*).[24] The poet Torquato Tasso defended play as a necessary diversion from the effort required by both the active and the contemplative lives.[25] Even the reforming Bishop Carlo Maria Bascapè, whose critique of Carnival will be discussed in Chapter 6, was aware of the need for 'a little relaxation' (*un poco di ristoro*) before the privations of Lent. The idea of recreation included music, especially making music. For this reason, the composer Orazio Vecchi called his book of madrigals and other songs 'A Collection of Various Forms of Recreation' (*Selva di Varia Recreazione,* 1595).

An inscription on an obelisk in the gardens of Bomarzo, described in Chapter 5, sums up the argument in a few words: 'to relieve the heart' (*sfogare il core*). Giving the argument a political twist, Cosimo

---

[24] Quoted in Deborah Parker, 'Toward a Reading of Bronzino's Burlesque Poetry', *Renaissance Quarterly* 50 (1997), 1011–44, at 1011.

[25] George McClure, 'Women and the Politics of Play in Sixteenth-Century Italy', *Renaissance Quarterly* 61 (2008), 750–91, at 756.

de' Medici, Grand Duke of Tuscany, who was once advised to forbid revelry, thought it better to allow it in order to divert the Florentines from thoughts of rebellion. Revelry was what a later generation, that of the industrial revolution, would call a 'safety-valve'. Today, unconsciously following the metaphor of the bowstring, we still speak of relaxing 'tension'.[26]

Some individuals saw both sides of the argument. A well-known example is that of Girolamo Cardano, the physician, mathematician and astrologer known as 'the gambling scholar'. His book on playing with dice, left unpublished in the author's lifetime, combined a treatise on the mathematics of probability with a manual for gamblers, including advice on how not to be cheated. Cardano's book also included what we would call a cost–benefit analysis. For example, he defended playing at cards and dice because it offered relief from grief and anxiety, but, on the other hand, he admitted that these games wasted time that might have been spent on more fruitful activities. Cardano extended his analysis from dice to other fields of play, and distinguished between different groups of players, especially the young and the old. For example, he suggested that 'gambling is proportionately less of a reproach to boys, young men, and soldiers'.[27]

---

[26] Norbert Elias and Eric Dunning, *Quest for Excitement: Sport and Leisure in the Civilizing Process* (Oxford, 1985); Alan Dundes and Alessandro Falassi, *La Terra in Piazza: An Interpretation of the Palio of Siena* (Berkeley, CA, 1975), 143.

[27] Ore, *Cardano*; David Bellhouse, 'Decoding Cardano's *Liber de Ludo*', *Historia Mathematica* 32 (2005), 180–202.

Play: For and Against

The Serio-Comic

The difficulty of defining the frontier between the serious and the comic was discussed earlier in the context of jokes that might or might not give offence. Some contemporaries explored this frontier in a philosophical manner. As the humanists well knew, the idea of the 'serio-comic' (in Greek, *spoudogeleion*) or 'playing seriously' (*serio ludere*) went back to the classical antiquity that they so much admired, to the laughing philosopher Democritus, for instance, to Plato and to Cicero.[28] Giordano Bruno compared himself to Democritus and claimed that his play 'The Ash Wednesday Supper' mixed the philosophical with the comic.

The variations on this theme might be described as a Renaissance theory of games. Ficino's remarks on the topic were quoted earlier in this chapter and might be juxtaposed to those of an Italian disciple of the German philosopher Nicholas of Cusa (1401–64): 'Play this game, but not in a childish manner' (*Luditer hic ludus: sed non pueriliter*). This text has been interpreted as a reference to the ancient Greek cult of Dionysus, the god of wine and festivities, symbolized by a child playing dice in the cosmic game of creation.[29]

---

[28] A (more or less) serious study of this topic is much needed. For parts of the story, see Edgar Wind, *Pagan Mysteries in the Renaissance* (Oxford, 1958), 179ff.; Thomas DaCosta Kaufmann, 'Arcimboldo's Serious Jokes', in Karl-Ludwig Selig and Elizabeth Sears (eds.) *The Verbal and the Visual* (New York, 1990), 59–80; Ian Petru Culianu, *Iocari serio: scienza e arte nel pensiero del Rinascimento* (2003: Italian translation, Turin, 2017); R. D. Waddington, 'Serious Play: From Satyr to Silenus', in *Aretino's Satyr* (Toronto, 2004), 117–51.

[29] Giovanni Andrea Bussi, quoted in Nicholas of Cusa, *De ludo globi* (1463), discussed in Wind, *Mysteries*, 179–85. Cf. Henri Jeanmaire, *Dionysus* (Paris, 1951).

Serio ludere is an ambiguous phrase that describes both a playful attitude to life and a desire to wear one's learning lightly – or, as Umberto Eco, master of the art, put it, 'Let's joke, but seriously' *(scherzare, sì, ma seriamente)*. *Serio ludere* offers a key to understanding the manifold activities of the many literary and learned academies founded in Renaissance Italy, some of whose practices, as we saw in Chapter 1, were dismissed by later scholars as 'frivolous'. These academies will be discussed in more detail in the following chapter.

5
Who, Where and When?

As we saw in the previous chapter, the 'gambling scholar' Girolamo Cardano made distinctions between players from different social groups. In similar fashion, this chapter displaces attention from play to the players – amateurs and professionals, children and adults, men and women, individuals and groups. It also examines the context of play: the places and the seasons in which different activities most often occurred.

Professionals

To begin with the professionals: teachers of music, dance, riding and fencing, for instance, and especially entertainers. In the early sixteenth century, during the Venetian Carnival, professional entertainers – actors like Cherea, clowns like Zuan Polo, acrobats like Battistin – were involved in public festivities as well as putting on shows in private houses. Professionals who worked the whole year round included fools or buffoons.

At this time, as in the Middle Ages, in Italy as elsewhere

in Europe, no court was complete without one or more such fools.[1] They were often dwarves, a reminder that, as we saw earlier, physical deformities were commonly regarded as funny. The fools were objects of ridicule, but some of them, perhaps in self-defence, became masters of ridicule, and in a few cases their witty remarks as well as their performances gained them a place at court – in Ferrara, for instance, and in Mantua, in Rome and in Florence. In Mantua, Isabella d'Este, better known for her interest in Renaissance art and humanism, surrounded herself with dwarves and fools.[2] In Rome, Pope Leo X, another patron of art and humanism, employed a Dominican friar, Fra Mariano, as his court fool.[3] A few buffoons became famous in their day. At the court of Ferrara, there was Pietro Gonnella, whose portrait was painted by the French master Jean Fouquet.[4] In Florence, Grand Duke Cosimo de' Medici, who looks so serious in his portraits, employed no fewer than five buffoons, including Braccio and Barbino. The dwarf Braccio di Bartolo was known as 'Morgante', a reference to the giant in the poem by Luigi Pulci mentioned in Chapter 3. His portrait was painted by Bronzino. Braccio's rival, the dwarf Pietro Barbino, is commemorated by a statue in the Boboli Gardens, representing him naked, pot-bellied (like Bacchus or Carnival) and

---

[1] For a general survey, Enid Welsford, *The Fool* (London, 1935).
[2] Alessandro Luzio and Rodolfo Renier, 'Buffoni, nani e schiavi dei Gonzaga ai tempi d'Isabella d'Este', *Nuova Antologia* 118 (1891), 618–50, and 119, 112–46.
[3] Arturo Graf, 'Un buffone di Leone X', *Attraverso il '500* (1888: revised edn, Turin, 1916), 365–90.
[4] Carlo Ginzburg, *Jean Fouquet: ritratto del buffone Gonnella* (Modena, 1996).

Who, Where and When?

Figure 4 The dwarf Pietro Barbino
Source: ryarwood/Wikimedia Commons

riding on a tortoise.[5] Better known than any of these real individuals was a fictional buffoon, Bertoldo, the

---

[5] Detlef Heikamp, 'Nani alla corte dei Medici', in Anna Bisceglia, Matteo Ceriana and Simona Mammana (eds.) *Buffoni, villani e giocatori alla corte dei Medici* (Livorno, 2016), 41–67.

creation of Croce. Bertoldo is presented as a master of tricks (*astuzie*).[6] The frontier between the buffoon and the comic actor is impossible to draw. In Venice, leading figures on this frontier, playing to a wider public than the courts just mentioned, were Zuan Polo, who was also an acrobat; his son, known as *Cimador*; and Domenigo Taiacalze ('Cut-Hose'), whose nickname suggests that he worked as a tailor as well as an actor. All too little is known about this trio, apart from the fact that they performed in particular places on particular occasions. More is known, thanks to their writings, about Angelo Beolco (*Ruzzante*) and Andrea Calmo, both of whom were actors as well as playwrights.[7] Other popular performers were the 'singers of tales' (*cantastorie*) who improvised – or, more exactly, semi-improvised – their stories on public squares, and accompanied themselves on a stringed instrument known as a *cetra* ('zither') or a *lira di braccio* ('lyre'). They were also known as *cantimbanchi* ('singers on a bench'), since they stood on benches so that the crowd could hear them more clearly.

Besides performing, these singers sometimes sold texts of their own work and that of other poets. A few of them achieved fame in their own time – like Cristoforo, nicknamed 'Altissimo', who came from Florence, or Jacopo Coppa, who came from Modena.[8] A related group of

---

[6] Piero Camporesi, *La maschera di Bertoldo: G. C. Croce e la letteratura carnevalesca* (Turin, 1976).
[7] Linda L. Carroll, *Angelo Beolco (il Ruzante)* (Boston, MA, 1990); on Calmo, Kathleen M. Lea, *Italian Popular Comedy* (Oxford, 1934), 239–45; Ludovico Zorzi, 'Calmo, Andrea', in *Dizionario Biografico degli Italiani* (Milan), www.treccani.it/enciclopedia/andrea-calmo_.
[8] Luca Degl'Innocenti and Massimo Rospocher, 'Street Singers: An Interdisciplinary Perspective', *Italian Studies* 71:2 (2016), 149–53, https://

Who, Where and When?

performers were the 'charlatans' (*ciarlatani*), who set up a stage on the piazza (most famously, Piazza San Marco in Venice) and presented what might be called a 'theatre of healing', apparently curing wounds on stage before selling their supposedly wondrous medicines, together with soap, perfume and other products. Coppa did this too.[9]

Comic texts also flowed from the pens of professional writers, many of them at work in Venice, the centre of Italian publishing at this time. These writers were known as *poligrafi* because they wrote so much and on so many subjects, serious as well as playful. They included Dionisio Atanagi, who edited a collection of facetious letters; Lodovico Dolce, who wrote comedies and comic poems; Lodovico Domenichi, who wrote comedies and edited a jestbook; Antonfrancesco Doni, who wrote playful dialogues and a commentary on the nonsense verse of Burchiello; Ortensio Lando, who published paradoxes, comic dialogues and funeral orations for animals; and Francesco Sansovino, who was, among many other things, the author of some comic poems. To survive economically, the *poligrafi* and the firms who printed and sometimes commissioned their work had to be successful in guessing what would sell, so their comic productions must have responded to public demand.

---

doi.org/10.1080/00751634.2016.1175713; Innocenti and Rospocher, 'Urban Voices: The Hybrid Figure of the Street Singer in Renaissance Italy', *Renaissance Studies* 33 (2018), 17–41, https://doi.org/10.1111/rest.12529; Innocenti, '*Al suon di questa cetra*': *ricerche sulla poesia orale del Rinascimento* (Florence, 2016).

[9] David Gentilcore, *Medical Charlatanism in Early Modern Italy* (Oxford, 2006).

Amateurs

Amateurs also played an important role in the playful practices described in earlier chapters. For most people, most of the time, access to professional spectacles and performances was limited. For this reason, 'Do It Yourself' entertainment was more important in Renaissance Italy than it became later. For example, amateur music-making was commonplace, especially playing the lute or singing, often for three or four voices. Printed music, available in Italy from the year 1501 onwards, made it easier than before for amateurs to widen their repertoire.[10]

Amateur theatricals were widespread for similar reasons. Writing comedies was a playful exercise in which diplomats, courtiers, secretaries and humanists all indulged: Ariosto in Ferrara, Bibbiena in Urbino, Machiavelli and Varchi in Florence. Leonardo in Milan and Giorgione in Venice took time from their art to compose, sing and play instruments. Michelangelo, Raphael and Bronzino wrote sonnets and other poems. Writing verse was a commonplace activity. Besides ruling Florence, Lorenzo de' Medici wrote Carnival songs and a poem entitled 'The Drinkers' (*I Beoni*). 'Writing verse' (*versificare*) was the name of a game described in Girolamo Bargagli's well-known dialogue. Much verse was occasional, taking the form of a letter to a friend or a comment on a recent event, giving the impression of spontaneity – though we need to remember that such an impression formed part of the negligence (*sprezzatura*) recommended by

---

[10] Nanie Bridgman, *La vie musicale au quattrocento* (Paris, 1964), 192–5.

Castiglione and that it might be the result of hours of study.[11]

Play and games were particularly important for nobles. They demonstrated what the American sociologist Thorstein Veblen called 'conspicuous leisure'. Losing wagers was a way of showing a noble indifference to money. As Aretino suggested, 'To risk nothing is a thing for a man worth nothing.' For nobles, it was also important to demonstrate self-control while playing, thus distinguishing themselves from common players who became angry and violent when they lost.[12]

The Clergy at Play

In this context, the important role of the clergy in various forms of play, at least until the middle of the sixteenth century, may come as a surprise to many readers. As in the late Middle Ages, preachers enlivened their sermons with comic anecdotes. During Carnival, some of the clergy wore fancy dress and, as a famous passage in the *Book of the Courtier* (book 2, ch. 87) reminds us, they threw eggs at the crowd just like everyone else. According to the Florentine writer Grazzini, at Carnival, 'Friars play ball with each other, perform comedies, and dressed in costume, sing, dance and play instruments.' Even nuns participated in the festivities.

Among the writers discussed earlier, Leonbattista

---

[11] Laura Riccò, *Giuoco e teatro nelle veglie di Siena* (Rome, 1993), 46.
[12] Thorstein Veblen, *The Theory of the Leisure Class* (New York, 1899), 18–32; Jonathan Walker, 'Gambling and Venetian Noblemen, c. 1500–1700', *Past and Present* 162 (1999), 28–69, at 29n, 50; Guido Guerzoni, 'Playing Great Games: The *Giuoco* in 16th-century Italian Courts', *Italian History and Culture* 1 (1995), 43–63, at 53–4.

Alberti was officially a cleric. Ortensio Lando had been a friar before becoming a *poligrafo*. The humanist Claudio Tolomei ended his life as a bishop, Giovanni Della Casa as an archbishop, and Pietro Bembo as a cardinal, while Baldassare Castiglione was the Pope's ambassador to the Emperor Charles V. Three monks have an important place in the comic literature of the Renaissance: Teofilo Folengo, who wrote macaronic verse; Agnolo Firenzuola (later a secular priest), who wrote comedies and comic poems; and Adriano Banchieri, another author of comedies, as well as a musician and the abbot of a monastery near Bologna. As was noted earlier, a Dominican friar played the fool at the court of Pope Leo X. A parish priest near Florence, Arlotto Mainardi, became famous for his comic sayings and doings (*facezie*), which were collected and published after his death. Matteo Bandello, some of whose published stories reveal a Rabelaisian style of humour, was a priest in Milan before becoming a bishop in the south of France (Rabelais, too, was a member of the clergy). The author of the first printed guide to tennis, Antonio Scaino, was a priest in Ferrara. Presumably he rolled up his cassock to take part in the game.

Women at Play[13]

The role of women at this time was relatively passive in playful activities, as in many serious ones, often

---

[13] Virginia Cox, 'Renaissance Woman', in *A Short History of the Italian Renaissance* (London, 2015), ch. 6; Alessandro Arcangeli, 'Exercise for Women', in Rebekka von Mallinkrodt and Angela Schattner (eds.) *Sports and Physical Exercise in Early Modern Culture* (Abingdon, 2016), 147–64; Arcangeli, 'Genere dei giochi e giochi di genere nella cultura ludica del

Who, Where and When?

– though not always – confined to watching men in action. Upper-class women were among the spectators of jousts and tournaments, while a mock-battle took place in Florence in 1464 in honour of Marietta degli Strozzi, a girl from a leading family (in the same year, Marietta was involved in a snowball fight with some young men).[14] In the cities where the celebration of Carnival included a procession or parade of floats through one of the main streets, the role of women was to watch from their balconies.

Nevertheless, the exceptions to this rule of passivity were important ones. Even watching or listening could be active. A Flemish composer who listened to performances of *villanelle* in the palaces of aristocrats in Naples noted that some young girls laughed so 'uncontrollably and with such great cheer, that they had to be held up. Otherwise they would have fallen down from the pleasure they derived in hearing the songs.'[15] Princesses, prostitutes and widows all had more freedom than maidens and wives, while wives had more freedom than maidens. In a collection of stories published in 1609, the maidens, hearing that the company mean to speak 'freely' (*licenziosamente*), leave the room, but the married women remain.[16]

Rinascimento europeo', in Francesca Aceto and Francesco Lucioli (eds.) *Giocare tra Medioevo ed età moderna* (Treviso and Rome, 2019), 151–65.
[14] Richard C. Trexler, *Public Life in Renaissance Florence* (New York, 1981), 230.
[15] Ghiselin Danckerts, quoted in Donna G. Cardamone, 'A Colorful Bouquet of Arie Napolitane', *Recercare* 10 (1998), 133–50, at 135–6.
[16] Celio Malespini, *Duecento novelle* (Venice, 1609), quoted in Riccò, *Giuoco*, 125. Cf. Claude Bérard, 'Il spazio ludico femminile', in *Passare il tempo: la letteratura di gioco e di trattenimento dal 12 al 16 secolo* (Rome, 1993), 475–509.

Doctors recommended some forms of exercise for women, including the swing. Dancing – at least some forms of dance – was an approved form of recreation for respectable girls, like singing and playing instruments such as the harpsichord. Showing off the skills of these girls was a way of attracting potential husbands. Some aristocratic ladies were celebrated for their singing, including Beatrice d'Este in Milan, her sister Isabella in Mantua and, especially, Elisabetta Gonzaga in Urbino. Elisabetta also played the lute. A few women became professional singers, among them Laura Peverara, who came from Mantua and performed at the court of Ferrara.

Some ladies wrote poetry (notably Veronica Gambara and Gaspara Stampa), and even published it (Vittoria Colonna, Tullia d'Aragona and Laura Battiferri, for example).[17] Amateur theatricals offered active roles for women in the safety of the home, while professional actresses worked in the *commedia dell'arte* from the 1560s onwards. They included Lucrezia da Siena, Vincenza Armani and, most famously, Isabella Andreini, who married an actor and starred in performances by a troupe known as the 'Jealous Ones' (*Gelosi*).[18] In this respect, the situation in Italy was very different from that in Shakespeare's London, where female roles were played by boys.

Dancing was not the only way for ladies to keep physically active without danger to decorum. Upper-class women participated in hunts, and some were praised for their riding skills, among them the Duchess of Urbino

---

[17] Virginia Cox, *Women's Writing in Italy, 1400–1650* (Baltimore, MD, 2008).
[18] Robert Henke, *Performance and Literature in the Commedia dell'Arte* (Cambridge, 2002), 85–105.

Who, Where and When?

and Diana Saliceto Bentivoglio. According to the Duke of Milan, his young wife Beatrice d'Este, sister of Isabella, 'has developed a perfect passion for horsemanship, and is always either riding or hunting'.[19] At home in their palaces or villas, noblewomen played an early form of table-tennis (*pallamaglio di tavola*). According to Antonio Scaino, girls played football in Udine when he was young.[20]

Some women played an active role in the Venetian Carnival, according to the diary of the patrician Marin Sanudo. In 1525, for instance, 'no woman wore fancy dress, according to the decree' (*niuna femina stravestita iusta la crida*), implying that the practice was common enough to forbid. In 1529, some 'wild women' took part in a battle with wild men, and Sanudo noted that 'real women' took part.[21] Prostitutes took part in Carnival, and so did nuns. According to Antonfrancesco Grazzini, 'Even nuns are permitted to celebrate by dressing as men: velvet caps on their heads, tight-fitting stockings on their legs, and swords on their hips.'[22] As for noblewomen, when Countess Barbara Sanseverino visited the court of Ferrara at Carnival in 1577, she dominated the festivities. According to a report by the Florentine ambassador, she organized a game of *calcio* that included women, and planned a tournament in which she would personally take part.[23]

---

[19] Julia Cartwright, *Beatrice d'Este* (London, 1903), 81.
[20] Antonio Scaino, *Trattato del gioco della palla* (1555; English translation, *Scaino on Tennis*, London, 1951).
[21] Marin Sanudo, *I diarii*, 58 vols. (Venice, 1879–1903), vol. XXXVII, 639, and vol. XLIX, 422.
[22] Elissa Weaver, *Convent Theatre in Early Modern Italy* (Cambridge, 2002).
[23] Quoted in George McClure, 'Women and the Politics of Play in Sixteenth-Century Italy', *Renaissance Quarterly* 61 (2008), 750–91, at 765–6.

It was, however, in the sphere of what we call 'parlour games' (*giochi d'ingegno*) that women had most freedom, playing on more or less equal terms with men. A famous example of the ambiguity of their position comes from Castiglione's *Courtier*, where women dominate the framework but men virtually monopolize the dialogue. The text is presented as the record of a game played at the court of Urbino over successive evenings. It is the Duchess, Elisabetta Gonzaga, who presides over the proceedings, appointing a female deputy, Lady Emilia Pia, to organize the game. It is Emilia who asks for suggestions and then decides on a discussion of the perfect courtier. One might say that she is the director of the play. However, the main speakers in the dialogue are all male, while the ladies are described as listening, interjecting remarks only every now and then. The world of the *Courtier* makes an obvious contrast with the world of Boccaccio's *Decameron*, in which the ladies are in a majority and participate fully in the storytelling.[24]

In similar fashion to the game of the courtier, in the game of the ship (described in Chapter 2), the lady is in control – at the helm, one might say – but the men who try to show why they should not be thrown overboard are allotted most of the words. In other forms of play, however, whether guessing games, games of chance, board games or challenges to recall passages of poems by Petrarch or Ariosto, women competed on more or

---

[24] Thomas M. Greene, '*Il Cortegiano* and the Choice of a Game', in Robert W. Hanning and David Rosand (eds.) *Castiglione: The Ideal and the Real in Renaissance Culture* (New Haven, CT, 1983), 1–16; Marina Zancan, 'La donna e il cerchio nel *Cortegiano*', in Zancan (ed.) *Nel cerchio della luna* (Venice, 1983), 13–56; Giuseppe Mazzotta, *The World at Play in Boccaccio's Decameron* (Princeton, NJ, 1986).

less equal terms with men, taking 'opportunities to perform' in this 'arena for fame'.[25] Princess Leonora d'Este played chess, and the poet Torquato Tasso's two treatises on games discuss other female chess players, such as Margherita Bentivoglio.[26] Treatises on parlour games targeted women. Ringhieri, the author of 'A Hundred Games of Skill' (*Cento Giochi Liberali et d'Ingegno*, 1551), addressed the 'intelligent lady' (*donna d'ingegno*), and dedicated his treatise to the expatriate Florentine Catherine de' Medici. Girolamo Bargagli's 'Dialogue on Games' was also dedicated to a lady, another Medici – Isabella, daughter of the Grand Duke Cosimo. A manuscript of the dialogue was presented to her during the Carnival of 1564. The author mentioned other ladies in the text, and instructed them not to refrain, on grounds of morality, from participation in games or from speaking with men. Scipione Bargagli, author of 'The Entertainments' (*I trattenimenti*, 1587), a book of games for men and women, has been described as 'a champion for greater opportunities for women', 'even more than his brother'.[27] One reason for the appeal of games to women was surely the fact that, in games, 'the traditional and penalizing social hierarchies were temporarily erased'.[28]

---

[25] George McClure, *Parlour Games and the Public Life of Women in Renaissance Italy* (Toronto, 2013), xv.
[26] McClure, 'Women', 754, 756, 760.
[27] McClure, *Parlour Games*, 68. Cf. Elena Brizio, '*Il Dialogo de' Giuochi* by Girolamo Bargagli and the Women of Siena', *The Scholar and Feminist* 15 (2018), sfonline.barnard.edu/women-and-community-in-early-modern-europe.
[28] Guerzoni, 'Playing Great Games', 59.

Child's Play

Some of the late medieval friars who criticized play in general also discussed children's games. Whether they condemned or allowed them, they offer valuable evidence about the favourites. Roberto da Lecce, for instance, allowed boys to play ball. Giovanni Dominici criticized wooden horses, cymbals and gilded drums, as well as artificial birds (apparently the equivalent of later teddy bears). On the other hand, Dominici allowed competitions to see who could run fastest or jump highest, and he positively recommended imitating the priest saying mass.[29] As in the case of adults, the municipal authorities were particularly concerned with mock-battles, such as the *batagliole puerorum* prohibited in Turin in 1360. The violence of children and young men remained a problem throughout our period.[30]

In *La tipocosmia* (1561), Alessandro Citolini, a Protestant scholar living in exile in London, listed many games for boys but only three for girls: playing with dolls (*le puppe*), playing the gossiping godmother (*giucar a le comari*), and playing house (*le scodelle*, literally 'dishes'). A doll of the Christ child was a not uncommon gift to girls who were either about to be married or to enter a convent, a means of training in both motherhood and devotion.[31] It is safe to assume, though, that girls

---

[29] Giovanni Dominico, *Regola del governo di cura familiare*, ed. Donato Salvi (Florence, 1860).

[30] Alessandra Rizzi, *Ludus/ludere: giocare in Italia alla fine del medio evo* (Rome, 1995), 101; Ottavia Niccoli, *Il seme della violenza: putti, fanciulli e mammoli nell'Italia tra cinque e seicento* (Rome, 1995).

[31] Patricia Fortini Brown, 'Children and Education', in Marta Ajmar-Wollheim and Flora Dennis (eds.) *At Home in Renaissance Italy* (London, 2006), 136–43; Christiane Klapisch, 'Les saintes poupées: jeu et dévotion

and boys played some games together, such as blind man's buff (*Maria orba, mosca cieca*) and hide and seek (*sconder il vesco*). Young adults also played both games, a reminder that children's culture and adult culture were not so far apart at this time as they later became. Conversely, Carnival was for children as well as adults. Its importance for them was evoked by the Florentine writer Giambattista Gelli, remembering that 'to me, when I was a child, it seemed a thousand years between one carnival and the next'.[32]

Children with access to writing materials made drawings, one of which is represented in a well-known painting by Giovanni Francesco Caroto of Verona. They recited rhymes and songs, whether or not they shared them with adults. We may imagine children chanting the fifteenth-century political song, 'Brave Braccio conquers everyone / Pope Martin is not worth a farthing' (*Braccio Valente / Vince ogni gente / Papa Martino / Non vale un quattrino*).

Play Groups

Play both expresses and constructs group solidarity, whether between members of a more or less formal team, or participants in what some German scholars call 'communities of laughter' (*Lachgemeinschaften*).[33] As we have seen in the cases of Florence, Pisa and Venice, the solidarity between members of a particular quarter

---

dans la Florence du Quattrocento', in Philippe Ariès and Jean-Claude Margolin (eds.) *Les jeux à la Renaissance* (Paris, 1982), 65–80.
[32] Giambattista Gelli, *Capricci del Bottaio* (Florence, 1546).
[33] Werner Röcke and Hans Rudolf Velten (eds.) *Lachgemeinschaften: kulturelle Inszenierungen und soziale Wirkungen von Gelächter im Mittelalter und in der frühen Neuzeit* (Berlin, 2005).

of a city was reinforced – if not created – by competition with another quarter, whether in races or in fights.

A common term for a group engaged in play was the *brigata*, more or less a 'gang' (in the social, not the criminal, sense of the term). Boccaccio referred to the story-telling group whose activities frame the *Decameron* as a *brigata*, and both Bandello and Girolamo Bargagli follow his example by referring to their texts (one to his stories and the other to his dialogue) as the record – or at least as the result – of conversations among a festive group. Innocentio Ringhieri assumes that his instructions for playing various games will be read to a 'festive and affectionate *brigata*'.

Another word to describe a festive group was 'company' (*compagnia*), as in the case of the *Compagnie delle Calze* in Venice, groups of young men distinguished by their parti-coloured hose (*calze*), the equivalents of the striped blazers of later British sports clubs. These companies, which took fanciful names such as the 'Gardeners' (*Ortolani*) or the 'Eternal Ones' (*Sempiterni*), acted in the amateur theatricals already mentioned, especially at Carnival, and also provided music at feasts. Elsewhere in Italy, plays were performed by Carnival societies such as the 'Congregation of the Rustics' (*Congrega dei Rozzi*), a group of artisans from Siena whom Pope Leo X invited to Rome each year.[34]

All these groups, like the carnivalesque 'Abbey of Fools' (*Badia degli Stolti*) in Turin, were dominated by young adult males, usually but not always from the upper classes. The mock- and not-so-mock-battles

---

[34] Curtio Mazzi, *La Congrega dei Rozzi di Siena nel secolo XVI* (Florence, 1882).

Who, Where and When?

described earlier were probably dominated by the same group of young men, especially unmarried men. In the 'stick wars' of Venice, the leading participants were two occupational groups linked to two quarters (or in Venice, 'sixths', *sestieri*), the fishermen from Cannareggio and the ship-builders from Castello. Young adult males also dominated another form of playful sociability in Renaissance Italy: the academies.[35] Girolamo Bargagli was 20, for instance, when he entered the Academy of the *Intronati*. Giovanni Della Casa was 29 when he became a founder-member of the Academy of the *Vignaioli* in Rome. The unofficial leader of the group, Francesco Berni, was 35, while Annibale Caro was 25. Looking at a portrait of Caro, showing a white-haired man, probably in his sixties, dressed in black, with the cross of an order of chivalry hanging from his neck, it is difficult to imagine him as the author of the mock-commentary on the mock-eulogy of figs by his fellow-*vignaiuolo* Francesco Maria Molza. It is even more difficult to imagine Della Casa, who became Archbishop of Benevento, writing his comic-erotic verses in what he later called, with some exaggeration, his 'adolescence'.

The academy was a new kind of institution, though inspired by Plato's academy in Athens. The most famous example of this inspiration comes from fifteenth-century Florence, although this Platonic Academy was less formal than the sixteenth-century academies described

---

[35] David Chambers, 'The Earlier "Academies" in Italy', in Chambers and François Quiviger (eds.) *Italian Academies of the 16th Century* (London, 1995), 1–14; Simone Testa, *Italian Academies and their Networks, 1525–1700* (Basingstoke, 2015); Jane E. Everson, Denis V. Reidy and Lisa Sampson (eds.) *The Italian Academies, 1525–1700: Networks of Culture, Innovation and Dissent* (2016).

above. This later type of academy might be described as a discussion group that was also a social club, with a fixed membership, officers – such as a prince, consul or councillors (*consiglieri*) – a name, a device *(impresa)* and certain social rituals. As in the case of games, academies exemplified the principle of the temporary equality of participants, reinforced by the custom of each member taking an academic name – in other words, a new identity. For example, members of the Academy of the *Intronati* (the 'Thunderstruck') of Siena included *il Stordito*, *il Cieco*, *il Sodo* and *il Scacciato* (respectively, the 'stunned', 'blind', 'solid' and 'chased out').

Academies proliferated in Italy in the sixteenth and seventeenth centuries. As we saw earlier, the scholars who discussed these academies in the eighteenth and nineteenth centuries tended to dismiss them for their frivolity and their ridiculous names. The names – which included the 'Sleepy Ones' of Genoa, the 'Eccentrics' of Perugia, the 'Humourists' of Rome and many more – were often self-mocking, like the names of many individual members. They were surely intended to show that the academicians, generally noblemen, carried their learning lightly and avoided pedantry.

Some academic activities were perfectly serious. The 'Lynxes' (*Lincei*), for instance, devoted themselves to 'natural philosophy' (in other words, 'natural science'), while the 'Bran' (*Crusca*) studied the Italian language. Their device was a sieve, symbolizing their intention to separate the linguistic wheat from the chaff. Members of academies often delivered or listened to lectures. A famous series of lectures on poetry and philosophy was given at the Florentine Academy by the humanist Benedetto Varchi.

Who, Where and When?

Many academies also had a lighter side, which came to the fore during Carnival. It is surely no accident that Scipione Bargagli, a writer on games, was also the founder of an academy, 'The Inflamed Ones' (*Accesi*). It was not uncommon for academies to perform plays (members of the *Intronati* of Siena even wrote some plays together). Two Roman academies, the *Accademia della Virtù* and the 'Wine-makers' (*Vignaioli*), were famous for the recital of comic verse, as well as for eating and drinking. In Florence, members of the Academy of 'The Wets' (*Humidi*) delivered burlesque lectures. In Milan, the members of the *Accademia della Valle di Bregno*, over which the painter Gian Paolo Lomazzo presided with the title of 'Abbot', gave themselves comic names and, as was noted in Chapter 2, spoke dialect.[36] The mock-eulogies and mock-commentaries by Caro and his colleagues in the *Vignaioli* fit comfortably into this context of erudite sociability, in which rivalry and wine inspired flights of fancy and creativity.

In short, 'playing seriously' (*serio ludere*) might have been the motto of most academies. The motto actually appears in the title of a collection of emblems published by Achille Bocchi, a professor at the University of Bologna and himself the founder of an academy, the *Bocchiana*.[37]

Playgrounds

The second of the three questions to which this chapter responds is: where did play happen? Courts have been

---

[36] J. B. Lynch, 'Lomazzo and the Accademia della Valle di Bregno', *Art Bulletin* 48 (1966), 210–11.

[37] Achille Bocchi, *Symbolicarum quaestionum de universo genere quas serio ludebat libri quinque* (Bologna, 1555).

mentioned again and again already, and this is no accident. Since courtiers, male and female, were members of a leisure class, it is no surprise to find that they were often deeply involved with play. Indeed, remembering the sociologist Pierre Bourdieu's famous discussion of the ways in which different social groups try to distinguish themselves from one another, we might say that one function of games at court was to construct the court as a place distinct from the rest of society.[38]

As we have seen, the court of Ferrara, where the Este family ruled, was a leader in these activities, including tournaments, dances, music and the theatre. The court was the scene of what was apparently the first performance of an ancient Roman play since the end of the ancient world. The play, the *Menaechmi*, by Plautus, who was believed to have come from Ferrara, was performed in 1486. Two leading poets of the Italian Renaissance, Ariosto and Tasso, were later resident at the court and participated in its festivities. Ariosto's comedy *Cassaria* had its first performance there in 1509, like Tasso's *Aminta* (1573). Tasso also set his dialogue *Romeo*, a discussion of play, at the court in the year 1579.

Thanks to the aristocratic Este sisters, Beatrice and Isabella, daughters of the ruler of Ferrara, playful activities were encouraged at the courts into which they married, Milan and Mantua. One of Beatrice's practical jokes has already been discussed, and so has Isabella's penchant for dwarves and fools. In a later generation, the court of Mantua was the setting for an early performance of Battista Guarini's pastoral drama 'The

---

[38] Pierre Bourdieu, *La distinction* (Paris, 1979). Cf. Amedeo Quondam, 'Giochi di corte', in Aceto and Lucioli, *Giocare*, 87–112.

Who, Where and When?

Faithful Shepherd' (*Il Pastor Fido*) in 1598, and for one of the first operas, Claudio Monteverdi's *Orfeo* (1609). Another small court, Urbino, has recurred in these pages because it was the setting for Castiglione's playful book about the perfect courtier. At the court of Florence, the festivities for the wedding of Grand Duke Ferdinando de' Medici in 1589 included – besides football, a lion hunt, riding at the quintain and the famous naval battle in the flooded courtyard of Palazzo Pitti – the performance of two plays. One of them, *The Pilgrim*, a comedy by Girolamo Bargagli, was played by the famous amateurs from the Academy of the *Intronati*, while the other was acted by professionals, the equally famous *Gelosi*. In the intervals of *The Pilgrim*, spectators could watch and listen to musical *intermezzi*.[39]

Turning now to the city, we find that major festivals took over the central urban space and transformed it into a gigantic theatre. In Florence, Carnival included a parade of floats along the main streets of the city. The equivalent in Rome was the Corso, a central street which takes its name from its use as a track for Carnival races of both humans and animals. On the periphery of the city, the open space around Monte Testaccio was the locale for fights between armed men and bulls, at which injuries and even deaths were commonplace.[40] More specific sites of play included bridges (especially for mock-battles, as we have seen), churches (especially for religious plays) and taverns (for gambling). In

---

[39] Aby Warburg (1895: English translation, *The Renewal of Pagan Antiquity*, Los Angeles, CA, 1999).

[40] Martine Boiteux, 'Chasse aux taureaux et jeux romains à la Renaissance', in Ariès and Margolin (eds.) *Les jeux*, 33–54, at 35, 37.

Venice, specialized *ridotti* or *casini* catered for gamblers at the higher end of the market.[41]

The principal site of play was the piazza, which possessed – and indeed still possesses – what has been called 'theatrical potential'.[42] In Rome, for instance, Piazza Navona, which had once served as the locale for chariot races, became the scene of jousts and bullfights (*caccia tori*).[43] In Venice, Campo San Stefano was the place to watch riding at the ring, while Piazza San Marco and the adjoining Piazzetta provided locations in which to watch processions, wild animals, mock-battles and the performances of charlatans. In Florence, Piazza della Signoria was the scene of formal dances and political announcements.[44] Piazza Santa Croce was the place to see ritualized football, jousts and the hunting of wild animals, while Piazza San Martino was the place to hear singers of tales.

The countryside also offered locales for play, not only the village tavern (such as the *osteria* where Machiavelli played *tric-trac*), but also the villas and gardens of the upper classes. Villas were also associated with leisure (*ozio*), in all its senses, offering sites not only for study but also for recreations such as storytelling and conversation, as Boccaccio and Bandello bear witness – not to mention doing nothing, *il dolce far niente*.[45] In villages, neighbours, male and female, would meet in the house

---

[41] Walker, 'Gambling and Venetian Noblemen, c. 1500–1700'.
[42] Sharon T. Strocchia, 'Theaters of Everyday Life', in Roger J. Crum and John T. Paoletti (eds.) *Renaissance Florence* (Cambridge, 2006), 55–80, at 42.
[43] Boiteux, 'Chasse aux taureaux'.
[44] Stephen J. Milner, 'The Florentine Piazza della Signoria as a Practiced Place', in Crum and Paoletti (eds.) *Renaissance Florence*, 83–103.
[45] Hannibale Firmano, *Convito del primo d'Agosto* (Rome, 1558); Adriano Banchieri, *Trattenimenti da villa* (1630).

of one of them in the evening or the first part of the night for a *veglia* – a 'wake', but without a corpse – working with their hands while listening to stories. For the upper classes, a *veglia* meant a locale for conversation, games and plays. In Siena, where the tradition of the *veglia* was particularly strong, Girolamo Bargagli placed his dialogue on games in this setting.[46]

The grand gardens to be seen in Renaissance Italy were not only works of art, as Jacob Burckhardt might have said, but also arenas of play. Grottoes in particular were playful places, where visitors, as we have seen, might be the butt of the joke. A more pleasant surprise occurred when the bronze birds decorating a fountain suddenly burst into song, as might happen in the Villa d'Este at Tivoli.[47] Another surprise came from the sight of monstrosities, including giants and dwarves, who were perceived not only as frightening but also as grotesque (a term derived from 'grotto'). They fitted into a wild landscape of rocks and caves that – according to a speaker in a sixteenth-century dialogue on the villa – produced both 'horror' and 'delight' in the spectator.[48] They often included mazes, which began to be common in Italian gardens from the fifteenth century onwards. Architectural handbooks proposed and illustrated designs for these labyrinths, some of which were large and impressive, as in the garden of the Villa d'Este.[49]

---

[46] Girolamo Bargagli, *Dialogo dei Giuochi* (1572: ed. Patrizia Ermini, Siena, 1982); Riccò, *Giuoco*; Gherardo Ortalli, 'Sixteenth-Century Courts and Salons: *giochi di veglia*', *Ludica* 19–20 (2013–14), 61–86.

[47] Claudia Lazzaro, *The Italian Renaissance Garden* (New Haven, CT, 1990), 17.

[48] Bartolomeo Taegio, *La villa* (Milan, 1559).

[49] Lazzaro, *Italian Renaissance Garden*, 51–5, 137. Cf. Luigi Zangheri, *Pratolino: il giardino delle maraviglie* (Florence, 1979); Luke Morgan, *The*

Play in Renaissance Italy

As a case-study, let us focus attention on one Renaissance garden, Bomarzo, which readers are recommended to visit when they can. Bomarzo is a small town not far from Viterbo, where a member of a noble Roman family, Pier Francesco Orsini (known as 'Vicino') had an estate. From 1552 or earlier, until his death in 1585, Vicino filled an area of trees and rocks on his land, which he described as his 'little wood' (*boschetto*), with fountains, benches, urns and statues of gods, goddesses, giants, lions, bears, Pegasus, Cerberus, an elephant, a dragon and a tortoise, not to mention a house, a theatre and a temple. This 'Sacred Wood' (*Sacro Bosco*), evoking the sacred grove in Virgil's *Aeneid*, is a wild garden, very different from – indeed, opposed to – the tame or formal gardens of the earlier Italian Renaissance. For this reason, it is sometimes described as 'Mannerist'.[50]

Ever since the rediscovery and the restoration of the garden of Bomarzo in the mid twentieth century, scholars have been discussing its programme or meaning, including the problem whether it has a meaning at all.[51] What is clear, at least, is the playful nature of Orsini's wood, as well as of its owner, who was acquainted with a number of individuals discussed in earlier chap-

---

Monster in the Garden (Philadelphia, PA, 2016), 140, quoting Taegio, *La villa*; Paolo Carpeggiani, '"Giochi" nei Giardini dei Gonzaga', *Ludica* 19–20 (2013–14), 146–65.

[50] Hence the place of Bomarzo in Eugenio Battisti, *L'antirinascimento* (Milan, 1962), 126–33.

[51] Jacqueline Theurillat, *Les mystères de Bomarzo* (Geneva, 1973); Horst Bredekamp, *Vicino Orsini und der heilige Wald von Bomarzo* (Worms, 1985); Lazzaro, *Italian Renaissance Garden*, 121–30; Maurizi Calvesi, *Gli incantesimi di Bomarzo* (Milan, 2000); Anne Bélanger, *Bomarzo ou les incertitudes de la lecture* (Paris, 2007); Morgan, *Monster in the Garden*, 135–63.

Who, Where and When?

ters, among them Annibale Caro, Ludovico Domenichi and Francesco Sansovino. One message inscribed on a stone in the garden, 'just to relieve the heart' (SOL PER SFOGARE IL COR), may – or may not – describe the purpose of the display. So may another: 'Eat drink play' (EDE BIBE LUDE). Further inscriptions, some of which contradict one another, offer clues that tantalize anyone who tries to interpret the ensemble, and may well have been intended to tease them. One of them asks the visitor to say whether 'so many marvels were made by deceit or by art' (SE TANTE MERAVIGLIE SIEN FATTE PER INGANNO O PUR PER ARTE). We have returned to the recurrent theme of deceit as a form of play, or play as a form of deceit.

As we have seen, riddles and other enigmas were common forms of playfulness in Renaissance Italy. Two figures of Sphinxes not only testify to Orsini's interest in ancient Egypt, but may also be intended to warn the overconfident interpreter. Allusions are everywhere – to ancient philosophy, to Greek, Etruscan and Egyptian mythology, and to Dante's *Inferno* and Ariosto's *Orlando Furioso*. These allusions, like the inscriptions, undermine one another.

Like the local rocks from which the statues were made, some of the play at Bomarzo is rough. Two giants are fighting, or wrestling, while a dragon is attacked by lions. In an age in which bull-baiting was a common form of entertainment, especially in Rome during the Carnival, sculptures such as these were probably seen as delightful, like the entrance to a cave that took the form of a mouth of hell. The stone giants may be fearsome but they may also be friendly, in the manner of Pulci's 'Morgante' or the giants of Rabelais (an author whom Orsini is

Figure 5 Bomarzo dragon
Source: Daderot/Wikimedia Commons

known to have appreciated). The inscription around the mouth of hell, 'Abandon Care, all you who enter here' (LASCIATE OGNI PENSIERO, VOI CH'ENTRATE), parodies Dante's 'Abandon Hope' and welcomes guests into a cool spot for a picnic, stone table included.

All the same, beneath the pleasantries there lies something disturbing. The wood carries undertones of Dante's 'dark wood' (*selva oscura*). There are references not only to the Christian Hell but also to the pagan Underworld. The inscription that recommends eating, drinking and playing ends with the line, 'After death there is no pleasure' (POST MORTEM NULLA VOLUPTAS): a brutal form of the *carpe diem* motif evoked in a famous poem by Lorenzo de' Medici: 'Let whoever wishes, be happy / There is no certainty of tomorrow' (*Chi vuol esser lieto, sia / Di doman non c'e certezza*).

If the impact of the *boschetto* on the viewer may be

Who, Where and When?

summed up in a single word, it is one that occurs in another inscription: 'wonders' (*meraviglie*). Visitors are invited to look at 'strange beasts' (*strane belve*) and 'terrifying faces' (*faccie horrende*). These statues are expected to produce surprise, a raising of the eyebrows (evoked in another inscription), a brief moment of fear, or a gentle shock – more gentle, at any rate, than the fountains of Pratolino and its rivals which were described earlier. The hoped-for conclusion is that the sacred wood surpasses any possible competition, even from the seven wonders of the world, including the Colossus of Rhodes, to which one inscription refers. Another inscription proclaims that the wood 'resembles itself and nothing else' (SOL SE STESSO E NULL ALTRO SOMIGLIA). A contemporary visitor described the *boschetto* as an example of art competing with nature (*mostra di fare a gara con la natura*). Competition is, of course, an essential part of play.

Seasons of Play

Jacob Burckhardt devoted a chapter of his famous essay on the Renaissance to 'Society and Festivals', suggesting that, at this time, the festival was the location in which 'religious, moral and poetical ideas took shape'. Mikhail Bakhtin agreed, claiming that Burckhardt did not exaggerate the influence of the festival on the culture of the Renaissance. On the contrary, 'it was even greater than he thought'.[52] Work was forbidden, while

---

[52] Jacob Burckhardt, *Civilization of the Renaissance in Italy* (1860: English translation, London, 1944), 246; Mikhail Bakhtin, *Rabelais and his World* (1965: English translation, Cambridge, MA, 1968), 159.

other prohibitions – of gambling in public, for instance – might be lifted. Italian festivals became more elaborate in the fifteenth century, thanks to competition between cities.[53]

Major festivals included Christmas, Carnival, Easter and Corpus Christi. Christmas lasted for twelve days, and its conclusion, Twelfth Night, was a favourite occasion for games that told fortunes. The Carnival season came in two versions – long and short. The long Carnival ran from the feast of St Stephen on 26 December till the beginning of Lent, while the term 'Carnival' in the strict sense referred to its climax, a final week of increasing excitement in which 'Fat Thursday' (*Giovedì Grasso*) and Shrove Tuesday were particularly important, a final paroxysm before the sober days of Lent. Play revived at Easter, including the tradition of 'Easter Laughter' (*risus paschalis*) and the performance of plays.[54] In Rome, for instance, Passion plays were performed at this time by the Company of the Gonfalon.

Corpus Christi was another occasion for plays, in which the main religious theme was accompanied by comic scenes that might represent Jews or devils. It has been argued that the rituals of Corpus Christi represented the 'social body' as much as the body of Christ, so that cities were in some sense celebrating themselves.[55] It is surely no accident that one of the most sumptuous, as well as the best documented, of the Corpus Christi pageants in Venice was performed in 1606, when the city was under a papal Interdict. A religious festival

---

[53] Rizzi, *Ludus*, 47.
[54] Maria Caterina Jacobelli, *Il risus pascalis* (Brescia, 1990).
[55] Mervyn James, 'Ritual, Drama and Social Body in the Late Medieval English Town', *Past and Present* 98 (1983), 1–29.

Who, Where and When?

was deployed for political purposes, to encourage the solidarity of the community and to support Venetian independence from the Pope.[56]

The festivals in honour of patron saints may be interpreted in similar fashion. The feast-day of the patron of a major city was an occasion of collective rejoicing marked by processions, banquets – 'feasts' in the literal sense of the term – and playful events such as races. In Florence, for instance, the feast of St John the Baptist, the principal patron and protector of the city, was a particularly splendid occasion. Its importance for the inhabitants was vividly described by one of them around the year 1400: 'You see the whole city involved in preparing for the feast, as if they had nothing else to do in the months leading up to the great day.'[57]

Besides the regular seasonal festivals, there were festivals marking special occasions such as victories, the election of a new pope or the formal entry into a city by an important figure such as the Emperor Charles V, who arrived in Bologna in 1530 for his coronation. The day was declared a holiday, fountains ran with wine instead of water, and balconies were crowded with spectators waiting for the processions and parades.[58]

Festivals had two sides: a serious side, which might be described as Apollonian; and a playful side, the Dionysian, linked to feasting, drinking, sex and violence. The Apollonian side more or less coincided with what

---

[56] Edward Muir, *Civic Ritual in Renaissance Venice* (Princeton, NJ, 1981), 223–30.
[57] Cesare Guasti (ed.) *Le feste di S. Giovanni Battista in Firenze* (Florence, 1884).
[58] Tiziana Bernardi, 'L'incoronazione di Carlo V a Bologna', *Quaderni Storici* 61 (1986), 171–200.

might be called the official 'core' of the festival, and the Dionysian side with its unofficial 'periphery'. In the case of the feast of St John in Florence, the centre of official events included the arrival of deputations from the subject towns – Pisa, Arezzo, Pistoia, Volterra, Cortona and so on – to offer tribute to the saint, and so to the city of which he was the patron. Around this core, however, there clustered a number of semi-official or unofficial entertainments, such as performances by jugglers, tightrope-walkers and giants (impersonated by men standing on stilts). They remind us that the feast of St John was a Christian replacement for a Midsummer festival, which still retained some elements, such as jumping over bonfires, from the original pagan one.[59]

Carnival

The greatest occasion for play in Renaissance Italy was Carnival.[60] Carnival in Venice followed a similar model of core and periphery to that of the feast of St John in Florence. The centre of the festival was Piazza San Marco and the accompanying Piazzetta, the site of traditional rituals such as the mock-execution of twelve pigs and a bull, whose carcasses were later given to the crowd. In the tradition of ancient rituals, this one was provided with its myth of origin. For the earliest surviving version of it, we are indebted to a foreigner who, as an outsider,

---

[59] Guasti (ed.) *Le feste di S. Giovanni Batista in Firenze* (Florence, 1884).
[60] Peter Burke, 'The World of Carnival', in *Popular Culture in Early Modern Europe* (1978: 3rd edn, Farnham, 2009), 255–86; Alessandro Arcangeli, 'El Carnaval, la risa y la cultura festiva en el Renacimiento', in Tomás Mantecón (ed.) *Bajtin y la historia de la cultura popular* (Santander, 2008), 131–44.

took nothing for granted. Arnold von Harff, a German nobleman who was passing through Venice in 1497 on his way to the Holy Land, recorded his question to a Venetian patrician about the reason for the execution of the twelve pigs and a bull. 'He told me that near Venice there was a country called Friuli, which was ruled by a patriarch', and went on to explain that the patriarch had attacked Venice, that he had been defeated and captured, and that the animals, which were sent to Venice every year as tribute, represented him and his twelve canons. The standard sixteenth-century guide-book to Venice tells the same story with the addition of the patriarch's name, Ulrich, and the date, the middle of the twelfth century.[61] As in the case of the Feast of St John in Florence, the celebration dramatized the power of the city and the submission of lesser cities to its rule.

By the sixteenth century, if not before, a number of less formal events had come to cluster around the tribute. This 'semi-periphery', as it might be called, included chasing bulls through the streets, riding at the ring, and the production of pageants on different themes. These 'triumphs' (*trionfi*), as Sanudo calls them, included a combat between four young men and four 'wild men' (1529); a devil tempting a pilgrim (1531); and pageants featuring classical gods and goddesses such as Neptune, Mars and Mercury (1528), or Venus and the planets (1587). An acrobat would walk a tightrope leading from the Campanile to the middle of Piazza San Marco.

Still further towards the periphery – if not on the fringe – were a number of less formal happenings both

---

[61] Arnold von Harff, *Pilgerfahrt*, ed. E. von Groote (Cologne, 1860), 52; Francesco Sansovino, *Venetia città nobilissima* (Venice, 1561).

on- and off-Piazza. Participants generally wore masks and they frequently wore fancy dress. From the later sixteenth century on, it became increasingly fashionable to dress up as characters from the *commedia dell'arte*, and the streets of Venice were filled with examples of the old man Pantalone, the cunning servant Zanni, and so on. Other recurrent figures were kings, beggars, peasants, madmen, Turks and Jews, the latter portrayed with long noses and sometimes in tears. Foreign visitors were impressed by the way in which the maskers, despite their numbers, not only dressed up, but also acted out their roles. As a background to these performances in public, one needs to imagine plays, banquets and balls in the palaces of patricians, and the sound of singing, fifes and trumpets both by day and by night. In other cities, the central events were somewhat different. In Florence, they included a parade of floats constructed by different guilds and featuring their members singing songs appropriate both to their trade and to the occasion. A surviving manuscript records the music for seventy-seven Florentine Carnival songs set for three or four voices.[62]

Major players might include personifications of Carnival as a fat man, reminiscent of Bacchus, eating and drinking and sometimes wearing a necklace of sausages. In Bologna in 1506, on the piazza in front of Palazzo Bentivoglio, a battle between Carnival and Lent took place, each with their supporters (*squadre*). A fat man on a fat horse represented Carnival, while an old woman on a thin horse represented Lent. After an hour of combat, Carnival was proclaimed the victor, and it was said that the laughter of the spectators could be

---

[62] Bridgman, *La vie musicale*, 159–60.

Who, Where and When?

heard all over the city. In Rome, in 1586, 'Carnival' made his entry through Porta del Popolo, in a cart drawn by four mules and loaded with food, including a large cauldron of macaroni.[63]

In contrast to the variety of the central events, the peripheral ones were much the same everywhere: eating, drinking, sexual intercourse, fighting, and throwing eggs, oranges or water at the crowd. A famous description of egg-throwing in Rome occurs in the *Book of the Courtier*, placed in the mouth of Bernardo da Bibbiena (book 2, ch. 87). Carnival was also a favourite time for *beffe* – witness an unusual case in the Governor's tribunal in Rome in 1551, after seven Jews had pretended to arrest a Neapolitan (at the time of their Carnival, Purim, not the Carnival of the Christians). This case might have been made into a comedy.[64]

Carnival was not only an occasion for plays, but itself a gigantic play, in which individuals wore masks and fancy dress and acted out their fantasies by means of the character that they chose to represent. Cross-dressing was permissible and foreign visitors regularly remarked on the – temporary – liberty of women that this custom allowed. A French visitor to the Carnivals of both Naples and Rome in the late sixteenth century, the Seigneur de Villamont, noted, besides the number of maskers on horseback, the costumes that imitated figures from the *commedia dell'arte*: Zanni, Pantalone and what the visitor called *stratulles* – in other words, the boastful soldier

---

[63] Details of the battle in Bologna come from a letter from Sabbadino degli'Arienti to Isabella d'Este. The Roman entry is described in Filippo Clementi, *Il carnevale romano* (Rome, 1899), 278.

[64] Thomas V. Cohen, 'The Case of the Mysterious Coil of Rope', *Sixteenth-Century Journal* 19 (1988), 209–21.

best known as Capitano, dressed on these occasions as a *stradiotto*, a mercenary from the Balkans.[65]

Capitano's bark was worse than his bite, but real violence was an inescapable part of Carnival. In Rome in 1499, masks were prohibited following attacks on individuals by masked men.[66] When the Jews raced along the Corso, they were pelted with mud and stones by the onlookers. In Rome, a substantial volume in the local archives records a trial for a murder that took place in the course of the Carnival of 1606 and involved some noblemen from Bologna, notably one of the Malvezzi family who was dressed as 'Zanni' at the time.[67] An English visitor in the late sixteenth century claimed that there were seventeen deaths on one day during the Carnival of Venice.[68] On 'Fat Thursday', in Treviso in 1615, a joke that caused offence provoked a battle between nobles and commoners that ended with five deaths.[69] Deaths during the celebrations were not confined to Italy, as a study of a sixteenth-century Carnival in the French town of Romans in France made abundantly clear.[70] Turning from physical to psychological violence, both formal and informal performances during Carnival were sometimes 'vehicles of protest', mocking the powers that be.[71]

[65] Jacques de Villamont, *Voyages* (Paris, 1595), book 1, chs. 24–5.
[66] Clementi, *Carnevale*, 102.
[67] Archivio di Stato, Roma, *Tribunale del Governatore, Processi, 17 secolo*, vol. LXVIII bis.
[68] Robert Dallington, *A Survey of the Great Dukes State of Tuscany* (London, 1605), 65. The year was 1596.
[69] Angelo Ventura, *Nobiltà e popolo nella società veneta nel '400 e '500* (Bari, 1964), 457n. Cf. Edward Muir, *Mad Blood Stirring: Vendetta and Factions in Friuli during the Renaissance* (Baltimore, MD, 1993).
[70] Emmanuel Le Roy Ladurie, *Le Carnaval de Romans* (Paris, 1979).
[71] Linda L. Carroll, 'Carnival Rites as Vehicles of Protest in Renaissance Venice', *Sixteenth-Century Journal* 16 (1985), 487–502.

Who, Where and When?

The meaning of Carnival has often been debated. For folklorists, it is or was a rite of spring, essentially concerned with fertility, symbolized by – among other things – eggs, sausages, obscene jokes, sexual activity and marriages (often celebrated at this time). For theologians, it is a form of preparation for Lent, a temporary indulgence in what would be prohibited between Ash Wednesday and Easter Sunday. For early modern participants, the opposition between Carnival and Lent (sometimes taking a dramatic form, as we have seen) was also important. Carnival and Lent were defined against each other.

Another central idea was that of 'the world upside down' (*il mondo alla rovescia*), a recurrent theme in popular culture in Italy, as elsewhere.[72] This world was enacted whenever men dressed as women or women as men, or the rich pretended to be poor while the (more or less) poor pretended to be rich. For this reason, Carnival was criticized, and for the same reason it was defended. It was declared to be a support for the social order by allowing temporary disorder, just as play in general was defended in similar fashion as a necessary form of relaxation, loosening the bowstring. As Roger Caillois would have said, Carnival exemplified (and still exemplifies, in Brazil and elsewhere) what he called 'vertigo', a collective excitement or ecstasy that reached its climax on Shrove Tuesday, just before Lent. It is only prudent to view the Carnivals of Renaissance Italy as palimpsests, texts with different layers of meaning – one of them uppermost in the minds of some participants or observers, another for others, and a third for later scholars.

[72] Giuseppe Cocchiara, *Il mondo alla rovescia* (Turin, 1963).

Carnival presented a concentration of ludic events, from fireworks to sword-dances, a microcosm of the world of play. Conversely, other ludic events may be regarded as 'carnivalesque'. It is therefore no surprise that individuals and groups who wished to reform popular culture, notably the Counter-Reformation clergy, should have concentrated their fire on this annual event, as we shall see in the following chapter.

6
New Trends

In this essay, the principal concern so far has been to reconstruct and interpret what might be called the 'play system' of Renaissance Italy – in other words, its repertoire, together with the conventions that players were supposed to respect. Structure has therefore been privileged over the changes that were taking place in the course of the period. In this chapter, however, as well as the brief epilogue that follows it, the emphasis will fall on change, including both gradual change over the long term (trends of which contemporaries were scarcely aware) and deliberate attempts to reform the culture, supported by some people and resisted by others. The principal attempt of this kind formed part of what historians have traditionally called the 'Counter-Reformation'.

The Counter-Reformation Campaign

As we saw in Chapter 4, in fifteenth-century Italy the friars, notably Bernardino da Siena and Savonarola, were already criticizing some forms of play from theological as well as moral points of view. Their criticisms were amplified from the middle of the sixteenth century onwards, the age of the 'Counter-Reformation', given this name because it responded to the Protestant Reformation of Luther, Calvin and Zwingli. The response combined the hunt for and the punishment of heresy with an attempt to raise the moral and educational standards of both the clergy and the laity. The Council of Trent, which was held in order to reform the Church from within, took place between 1545 and 1563 and marks a frontier zone between a more permissive and a stricter moral regime. Some individuals lived their lives on both sides of the frontier – Giovanni Della Casa, for instance, wrote poetry in his youth in the burlesque and sexually suggestive style of Berni. On the other hand, his *Galateo*, written in middle age and posthumously published in 1558, criticized the *beffa* and expressed the moral ideals of the new age.

The critique of play became more severe at this time, but also more precise, aimed at regulating or 'disciplining' particular forms of recreation. The leaders of the campaign against play in the later sixteenth century included not only its most famous protagonist, the ascetic Carlo Borromeo, Archbishop of Milan, but also Pius IV (Pope from 1559 to 1565); Gabriele Paleotti, the Archbishop of Bologna; the Jesuit Roberto Bellarmino; and Carlo Bascapè, who had been Borromeo's secretary before he became Bishop of Novara.

Like the Counter-Reformation in general, the campaign against play had two sides, negative and positive. The negative side consisted of prohibitions. In 1560,

New Trends

for instance, Pius IV forbade members of the laity to dress as clergy, to wear masks and to carry weapons in church.[1] In 1567, Bellarmino preached in Venice against Carnival and its dances and other 'follies', claiming afterwards that the sermon was well received and that a number of senators had tried to kiss his hand. In the 1570s, it was the turn of Carlo Borromeo – who had already denounced Easter plays for provoking laughter and instructed preachers not to tell funny stories – to go on the offensive. He now declared war on Carnival, opposing games, jousts, dances, plays, pageants, banquets and 'gluttony' (*crapule*), and persuading Pope Gregory XIII to ban these activities in Rome. Borromeo attacked comedies as 'nets' thrown out by the devil in order to entrap young people. In 1578, plays were denounced by Paleotti. In the same spirit, the Venetian Council of Ten prohibited plays in 1581. In Rome in 1586, Pope Sixtus V, more moderate than his predecessor Gregory, simply forbade Carnival revellers to throw eggs and oranges. However, bullfighting was banned by several popes in the later sixteenth century.

The work of Carlo Borromeo as a radical reformer was carried on by Bascapè, who issued his 'Announcement to Certain Parish Priests' (*Avviso a certi curati*) in 1598 against various 'abuses' of Carnival, among them burning certain images, announcing mock-marriages and organizing public feasts. In the same year, he published a letter denouncing dances. He returned to the assault in 1606 with his *Septuagesima* (referring to the third Sunday before Ash Wednesday, a time of Carnival), condemning the 'disorders of Carnival' or 'Carnival madness', such

---

[1] Filippo Clementi, *Il carnevale romano* (Rome, 1899).

as 'unnecessary banquets', 'immoderate expense' and 'immodest dances' (*danze licenziose*). He also advised the faithful to avoid plays and masquerades.[2] The reasons for all these prohibitions deserve some comments. One was to preserve holy things from contamination by profane ones. Hence the laity should not dress as clergy, while the clergy should not wear masks during Carnival (as even cardinals had been accustomed to doing). In Venice in 1616, for instance, the prior of the Ca' di Dio, an almshouse, was fined for holding the 'customary' masked ball.[3] For the same reason, preachers were forbidden to make jokes during their sermons, churches were ordered to be free from masks, the sacrament of marriage was not allowed to be mocked, and festivities were not permitted to encroach on the holy season of Lent, which Bascapè described as a time of 'modesty, devotion and penitence'.

Secondly, some jokes and games were viewed as blasphemous. For example, the Bishop of Cremona warned against joking about God, the saints or the Church (*non si burlare mai delle cose di Dio et suoi santi o della Chiesa*), since jokes might lead the jokers into heresy.[4] In the eyes of the reformers, even innocent joking seemed dangerous at a time when the ideas of Luther and Calvin were spreading in Italy. Thirdly, some playful practices were now viewed as pagan or even diabolical (*opere del Demonio*). Telling fortunes, for instance,

---

[2] These texts are reprinted in Fernando Taviani (ed.) *La Commedia dell'arte e la società barocca* (Rome, 1969).

[3] Deborah Howard, *Jacopo Sansovino: Architecture and Patronage in Renaissance Venice* (New Haven, CT, 1975), 118.

[4] Quoted in Gigliola Fragnito, *Rinascimento perduto: la letteratura Italiana sotto gli occhi dei censori (secoli XV–XVII)* (Bologna, 2019), 102.

was now reinterpreted as a pagan custom.[5] Girolamo Bargagli's dialogue, written in the 1560s and published in 1572, discussed games that should not be played, either because they were too sexually explicit or because they referred to religion. One of the speakers, whether mocking or serious, called this an 'index of prohibited games' on the model of the Roman *Index of Prohibited Books*.[6] A fourth reason was the traditional moral one offered by the friars. Carnival offers many occasions of sin, among them mortal sins such as gluttony, lust and anger. Carlo Borromeo was well aware of the danger of violence as well as sex during that period, and referred to 'brawls' (*risse*) and 'enmities' (*inimicizie*).

The clerical campaign against festivities was accompanied by a campaign against books. Bellarmino once remarked that 'I hardly read any book without wanting to censor it thoroughly' (*Io non leggo quasi libro nessuno, che non mi bastasse l'animo di fargli sopra una buona censura*).[7] The main target of the notorious *Index of Prohibited Books* was heresy, but action was also taken against works of entertainment.[8] For example, Spirto's popular guide to the game of telling fortunes was placed on the Roman *Index* in 1559. Obscenity was a major target. Aretino's notorious 'Lascivious Sonnets' (*Sonetti lussuriosi*) were prohibited as early as 1558. In his homilies, Carlo Borromeo warned his listeners

---

[5] Paolo Procaccioli, 'Verso L'indice e il decline del libro di sorti', in Francesca Aceto and Francesco Lucioli (eds.) *Giocare tra Medioevo ed età moderna* (Treviso and Rome, 2019), 133–44.

[6] Girolamo Bargagli, *Dialogo dei Giuochi* (1572: ed Patrizi Ermini, Siena, 1982), 84.

[7] Quoted in Fragnito, *Rinascimento perduto*, 126.

[8] There is a list of such works in Gigliola Fragnito, *Proibito capire: la Chiesa e il volgare nella prima età moderna* (Bologna, 2005), 201–2.

against 'obscene books', describing them as a dangerous 'weed' (*zizzania*).⁹ Paleotti disapproved of the stories of Bandello and even of a section of Ariosto's *Orlando Furioso* (though this poem was never banned).¹⁰ Bandello's short stories were expurgated in 1560. From the 1570s onwards, censorship became more severe. Boccaccio's *Decameron* was expurgated in the 1582 edition, not (as modern readers might have expected) for its sexual episodes, but for inappropriate references to the clergy, including an inquisitor.¹¹ The jokes in book 2 of Castiglione's *Courtier* were subjected to similar treatment in the expurgated edition of 1584.¹² The jestbooks of Arlotto Mainardi and Ludovico Domenichi, the letters of Andrea Calmo and the nonsense verses of Burchiello were not spared either. In 1586, the canon Tommaso Garzoni, himself a successful writer, condemned the comic works of Aretino and Berni because they were 'over the top' (*fuor di misura*).

The reforming offensive had a positive side as well as a negative one. In Milan, for example, Carlo Borromeo issued a circular ordering public processions with singing as an antidote to what he called the *baccanali del Carnovale*. Stone crosses were erected in different parts of the city in order to allow the faithful to follow the Stations of the Cross in the open air. Like Rome, Milan

---

[9] Borromeo's homily is quoted in Roberto Tessari, *La Commedia dell'arte* (Rome, 2013), 3.
[10] Paolo Prodi, 'San Carlo Borromeo e il cardinal Gabriele Paleotti: due vescovi della riforma cattolica', *Critica Storica* 3 (1964), 135–51; Fragnito, *Rinascimento perduto*, 101–2.
[11] Fragnito, *Rinascimento perduto*, 282–90.
[12] Andrea Sorrentino, *La letteratura italiana e il Sant'Ufficio* (Naples, 1935); Fragnito, *Rinascimento perduto*, 9, 82ff.

was becoming a 'ritual city'.[13] Religious plays performed in churches or on public squares replaced Carnival comedies. The fifteenth-century plays by Feo Belcari were revived, and new religious plays were performed, among them Simone Tubaldino's *Carnevale* (1591), showing the triumph of the Church over the world, the flesh and the devil.

It was at this time, ironically enough, that one of the Church's most playful saints, Filippo Neri, the founder of the Congregation of the Oratory, lived and worked in Rome. Filippo did not mind if young men made a noise outside – or even inside – his rooms. He was more than tolerant of their playfulness: he encouraged it, taking them to play ball, to play *piastrelle* (a game with tiles) or to play *ruzzola* (throwing a disc as far as possible).[14] According to witnesses at the investigation preceding his canonization, Filippo presented himself as 'a crazy old man', playing practical jokes on his followers, wearing his cloak inside out, shaving off half his beard or hopping and running in church. To escape from his growing reputation for sanctity, he showed himself to some visitors reading the jests of Arlotto Mainardi. 'Love and Joy' was his motto. One of his followers wrote a book entitled 'Philip, or Christian Joy'. Beatified in 1616 and canonized in 1622, Filippo Neri is perhaps the best example of a holy fool outside the Orthodox Church.[15]

---

[13] Adele Buratti (ed.) *La città rituale: la città e lo stato di Milano nell'età de Borromeo* (Milan, 1982).

[14] Antonio Cistellini, *San Filippo Neri*, 3 vols. (Brescia, 1989), vol. I, 98.

[15] Giovanni Incisa della Rocchetta (ed.) *Il primo processo per san Filippo Neri*, 4 vols. (Vatican City, 1957–63); Jean Vuaillat, *Saint Philippe Néri: le saint toujours joyeux* (Lyon, 1967); Paul Türks, *Philip Neri: The Fire of Joy* (1986: English translation, Edinburgh, 1995), 47, 98, 108, 124; Agostino Valier, *Philippus sive de christiana laetitia* (written 1591).

The Age of the Baroque

How effective were the prohibitions described above? Did Lent triumph at last in her battle with Carnival? As usual, it is difficult to give a simple answer to this kind of question, but if we follow the history of play into the seventeenth century, we find survivals alongside changes. Take the case of the late sixteenth-century popular poet, the prolific Giulio Cesare Croce of Bologna. Croce created two famous comic characters: the astute Bertoldo and his son, the simple Bertoldino. The author's virtuosity in parody and in playing with the Bolognese dialect is apparent in many of his works. Compared to his predecessors in the carnivalesque tradition, however, Croce's texts conspicuously avoid scatology, religion and radicalism. In these respects, they are signs of the times.[16]

Carnival did not disappear, although it may have become milder or more 'civilized' in the late sixteenth and early seventeenth centuries. At least some mock-battles became less violent, turning into a kind of ballet performed by armed men. In Florence, during the Carnivals of 1615 and 1616, battles in Piazza Santa Croce were organized on the themes of wars of love and beauty (*Guerra d'Amore, Guerra di Bellezza*). In Ferrara in 1635, the Carnival tournament also had a theme, 'Discord Overcome' (*La discordia superata*), suggesting once again that it was closer to theatre than to training for battle. In 1634, when Cardinal Antonio Barberini hosted a joust on Piazza Navona at a cost (including seating for spectators) of 60,000 *scudi*, the

---

[16] Piero Camporesi, *La maschera di Bertoldo: G. C. Croce e la letteratura carnevalesca* (Turin, 1976), 6, 187, 223.

event was again a kind of theatre.[17] In Palermo in 1648, an especially magnificent Carnival was organized by the viceroy to distract the people from memories of the revolt of 1647, although a diarist recorded the fear of disorder, since masked revellers might 'provoke a new tumult' (*suscitar nuovo tumulto*).[18] The English botanist John Ray, visiting Rimini in the early 1660s, discovered that 'Being Carneval time we found the Gentlemen here tilting. They ran not at one another but at a puppet or man of straw, *Bamboccio* they call it.'[19]

Comedies continued to be written and performed. In Florence, a comedy by Michelangelo Buonarroti the younger, 'The Pastime' (*Il passatempo*), was performed in the Palazzo Pitti in 1614. Three artists regularly wrote and acted in plays for the Roman Carnival: Salvator Rosa, Gianlorenzo Bernini and Giovanni Briccio, who was also a singer and the author of a *Lament of the Jews during Carnival*. The races continued: a race of naked hunchbacks was organized in 1633, while the race of Jews was not abolished until 1668.

As for the role of the clergy, the tradition of Arlotto Mainardi and other light-hearted clerics was carried on by Adriano Banchieri, a Benedictine monk who was active as a musician. Banchieri was also a writer of comedies and other works of entertainment, such as the 'Discourse on How to Escape the Idleness of Summer' (*Discorso per fuggir l'ozio estivo*, 1622). Sicilian priests

---

[17] Martine Boiteux, 'Carnaval annexé', *Annales ESC* 32 (1977), 356–77.
[18] Giuseppe Pitrè, *Usi e Costumi del popolo siciliano*, 4 vols. (Palermo, 1889), vol. I, 4, 10.
[19] John Ray, *Observations Topographical, Moral and Physiological* (London, 1673), 379.

continued to participate in Carnival.[20] Had he survived into the seventeenth century, Carlo Borromeo would not have been amused. References to the lower bodily stratum declined, however, while the *beffa*, passing through what one scholar calls a 'crisis', became more civilized and less funny. An early example of the new regime of humour comes from a collection of stories, the *Diporti*, by the composer, poet and playwright Girolamo Parabosco – a relatively mild *beffa* in which 'a large jar of water and hot ash' falls on the head of a lover as he arrives at the house of his lady.[21] There seems to have been a shift among the upper classes from dirty jokes (at least in mixed company) to wit and verbal humour. The seventeenth-century rhetorician Emmanuele Tesauro expressed a new ideal of elegance, dismissing 'popular jokes' (*facetie popolari*). He did not reject the *beffa* altogether, but he was much more interested in wordplay than in other forms of humour.[22] In this respect, he was a typical representative of the cultural movement we now call 'baroque'. The baroque obsession with wordplay may have been a form of psychological compensation, a reaction to the shrinking of the domain of the comic.

Another form of compensation was the rise of the caricature, which was invented in the early seventeenth century in the circle of the painters Annibale, Agostino and Ludovico Carracci. In other words, it was the work

---

[20] Pitrè, *Usi e Costumi*, vol. I, 16.
[21] André Rochon (ed.) *Formes et significations de la beffa*, 2 vols. (Paris, 1972–5), vol. I, 179–202.
[22] Emanuele Tesauro, *Il cannocchiale aristetolico* (1654: new edn, Turin, 1670), 38, 223, 583ff., 682; Mario Zanardi, 'Metafora e gioco nel Canocchiale aristotelico', *Studi Secenteschi* 26 (1985), 25–99.

New Trends

of artists famous for their classicism, suggesting that they needed some respite from idealization, while earlier forms of comic relief were now denied them.[23]

The mock-epic probably flourished for the same reason. The most famous example is 'The Robbery of the Bucket' (*La Secchia Rapita*, 1622 by Alessandro Tassoni, but there are others. *La Moscheide* (1623) by Giovanni Battista Lalli featured 'Domitian the fly-killer'. Another example is 'The Comic Iliad' (*L'Iliade Giocosa*, 1653) by the Venetian patrician Gianfrancesco Loredan.[24]

Codification and Separation

Some changes in the 'play system' of Renaissance Italy happened more slowly than the ones that the reformers attempted to impose, but they may have been equally important in the long run. This section will discuss two trends, both of them visible in Italy at this time but not unique to it: codification and separation.

Play was increasingly subject to rules, thus moving towards our own concept of 'sport'.[25] The printed book played an important role in this development. As we have seen, a series of treatises on different forms of play were published in Italy, beginning in the mid fifteenth century with books teaching the art of dancing,

---

[23] Ernst Kris, *Psychoanalytic Explorations in Art* (London, 1953), chs. 6–7; Irving Lavin, 'Bernini and the Art of Social Satire', *History of European Ideas* 4 (1983), 365–78.
[24] Alberto Asor Rosa and Salvatore S. Nigro, *I poeti giocosi dell'età barocca* (Bari, 1979).
[25] Rebekka von Mallinkrodt and Angela Schattner (eds.) *Sports and Physical Exercise in Early Modern Culture* (Abingdon, 2016).

Play in Renaissance Italy

and followed by guides to horsemanship, tennis, fencing, gymnastics and football. These treatises – part of a much larger group of 'how to do it' books on cooking, carving and many other practices – are not only valuable sources for the reconstruction of the play system, but also testimonies to the process of codification.[26] In the case of some parlour games, it would have been difficult, if not impossible, to play them without a treatise at hand for ready reference. More generally, the treatises encouraged people to play according to generally accepted rules, which were standardized to an extent that would have been impossible before the invention of printing. It has been argued that the systematization of different forms of play, the increasing concern with rules, made play less playful.[27] The professionalization of certain games pushed in the same direction, giving a new meaning to the old phrase *giocare serio*.

The 'separation' between forms of play includes the games that adults increasingly abandoned to children, from snowball fights to blind man's buff. However, the main point of using the term is to refer to a gradual trend that I have described elsewhere as the 'withdrawal' of the European upper classes (and, later, the middle classes) from participation in what came to be known

---

[26] Carlo Bascetta, 'Codes verbaux de jeu et littérature sportive italienne', in Philippe Ariès and Jean-Claude Margolin (eds.) *Les Jeux à la Renaissance* (Paris, 1982), 95–107; Rudolph M. Bell, *How To Do It: Guides to Good Living for Renaissance Italians* (Chicago, IL, 1999); on Ringhieri, Gherardo Ortalli, 'Sixteenth-Century Courts and Salons: *giochi di veglia*', *Ludica* 19–20 (2013–14), 61–86, at 66.

[27] John McClelland, 'Sport and Scientific Thinking in the Sixteenth Century: Ruling Out Playfulness', *Ludica* 19–20 (2013–14), 134–45.

New Trends

as 'popular culture'.[28] Around the year 1500, in Italy as elsewhere, these forms of culture belonged to everyone, either as participants or spectators. Members of all social groups gambled, and males, whatever their status, might participate in competitions to show strength and skill. In Castiglione's dialogue on the perfect courtier, one of the speakers, the Lombard Gasparo Pallavicino, pointed out that the gentlemen from his part of the world danced with peasants and competed with them in wrestling, running, jumping and throwing an iron bar. In Venice, as late as the 1580s, some young patricians participated in the 'stick wars'.[29] Carnival was for everyone, like the piazza where so many carnivalesque events took place. As Bakhtin put it, the 'Carnival square' was a 'symbol of communal performance'.[30]

Despite these examples of continuity, a process of separation was taking place. In the fifteenth century, court dances were becoming distinguished from popular dances.[31] During Carnival, some plays might be performed in the private houses of the upper classes. Public space was sometimes privatized, taken over by the upper classes for a particular event. This is what happened to Piazza della Signoria in Florence in 1431, when the square was turned into a ballroom by a patrician family whose daughter, Alessandra de' Bardi, was the belle of

---

[28] Peter Burke, *Popular Culture in Early Modern Europe* (1978: 3rd edn, Farnham, 2009), 366–80.
[29] Robert C. Davis, *The War of the Fists: Popular Culture and Public Violence in Late Renaissance Venice* (New York, 1994), 131.
[30] Baldassare Castiglione, *Il Cortegiano* (1528: ed. Bruno Maier, Turin, 1964), book 1, ch. 10; Mikhail Bakhtin, *Problems of Dostoyevsky's Poetics* (1929: English translation, Manchester, 1984), 124.
[31] Nanie Bridgman, *La vie musicale au quattrocento* (Paris, 1964), 62.

the ball.[32] In Rome in 1540, Pope Paul III, a member of the Farnese family, organized a bullfight for his guests by taking over the piazza in which his family palace was situated.[33]

Gradually, thanks at least in part to a general reform of popular culture by Catholics and Protestants alike, the play system of the elite was diverging from that of ordinary people – artisans and peasants and their wives and children. Returning to Castiglione's dialogue, another speaker, the Genoese patrician Federico Fregoso, argued that it was indecorous for a gentleman to participate in a rustic festival (*una festa di contado*), among common people (*gente ignobile*). A generation later, Giovanni Della Casa, who was a patrician as well as an archbishop, criticized buffoonery in his *Galateo* (1558) as conduct unbecoming a gentleman. Men from all social groups continued to gamble, but by the early seventeenth century nobles, at least in Venice, placed their bets in the specialized locales known as *ridotti* or *casini*.

It was Fregoso's opinion that generally prevailed in the later sixteenth century. In Bargagli's dialogue on games, one speaker argued that it was unseemly for nobles to play games that involved getting their faces dirty or hitting one another with sticks. That should be left to rustics.[34] We might speak – and one scholar has written – of a process of 'ennobling', the deliberate refinement

---

[32] Vespasiano da Bisticci, *Vite di Uomini Illustri* (Florence, 1859), 'Alessandra de' Bardi'.
[33] Martine Boiteux, 'Chasse aux taureaux et jeux romains à la Renaissance', in Ariès and Margolin (eds.) *Les jeux*, 33–54, at 39.
[34] Quoted in Laura Riccò, *Giuoco e teatro nelle veglie di Siena* (Rome, 1993), 44.

of popular games such as telling fortunes at Epiphany in order to make them fit for elites, in particular for noble ladies, or their replacement by games of a different kind. One author of the time, Pietro Fortini, referred to this process with the verb *dirozzare* ('to polish what is rough').[35] Another, Bartolomeo Arnigio, gave his treatise on games the sub-title of 'the reformed customs of human life' (*gli ammendati costumi dell'humana vita*) and praised the forms of play that exercised the wit, readiness, knowledge and memory of the participants.[36]

These changes, though certainly significant, were minor ones compared with the transformations of play in Italy and elsewhere between the eighteenth and the twenty-first centuries, transformations that will be sketched in the epilogue.

---

[35] Riccò, *Giuoco*, 111; Fortini, quoted at 55.
[36] Arnigio, quoted in Riccò, *Giuoco*, 101.

7
Epilogue: Beyond 1650

As a cultural historian, my main concern in this book has been to show the differences between the playfulness of the Renaissance and that of the present, viewing the past as a 'foreign country' with different customs from our own. I have presented Renaissance Italy as a particular culture, with its own patterns of work and play. For example, while competition can be found everywhere, Italians of this period, like ancient Greeks, seem to have suffered from an obsessive need to win, whether by force, skill or deceit.

It is time to situate the culture of Renaissance Italy in a longer period and a wider space than has been discussed so far. Italy at this time was one example among many of a pre-industrial society, or a cluster of pre-industrial societies, with patterns of both work and play that were very different from its industrial and post-industrial successors.

Epilogue: Beyond 1650

The Invention of Leisure

In the play system of pre-industrial societies, the main division of activities was one between everyday time and the time of festivals. A new form of separation, increasingly important from the eighteenth century onwards, divided work from 'free time' or 'leisure' in the evening, at weekends, and on holiday (the regular 'holidays' that have replaced the irregular 'holy days' of pre-industrial times).[1] The regular alternation of work and leisure was better suited to the rhythm of production in factories and was itself a product of industrial capitalism. The new idea of 'leisure' was related to the older idea of *ozio* but was not identical with it, since it came to be viewed as a right and to include everyone (at least in principle), while it lacked the earlier associations of *ozio* with both study and idleness.[2]

These changes were sometimes slow to take effect. In Italy, the industrial revolution did not begin till the 1890s and was limited to three northern cities: Milan, Turin and Genoa. Pre-industrial festivals and traditional forms of playfulness survived, especially in the countryside and the south. Hence, it was possible for folklorists such as Pitrè to write books about traditional popular Sicilian customs and festivals, or, even after the Second

---

[1] Wolfgang Nahrstedt, *Die Entstehung der Freizeit* (Göttingen, 1971).

[2] Edward Thompson, 'Time, Work-Discipline and Industrial Capitalism' (1967: repr. in *Customs in Common*, London, 1993, 352–403); Brian Vickers, 'Leisure and Idleness in the Renaissance: The Ambivalence of *Otium*', *Renaissance Studies* 4 (1990), 1–37; Peter Burke, 'The Invention of Leisure in Early Modern Europe', *Past and Present* 146 (1995), 136–50; Alessandro Arcangeli, *Recreation in the Renaissance: Attitudes Towards Leisure and Pastimes in European Culture, 1350–1700* (Basingstoke, 2003).

World War, for anthropologists to record rural festivals in which the villagers still re-enacted the trial, execution, burial and testament of Carnival.[3] Some traditions – survivals or inventions – were, and are, not confined to the countryside. The success of Silvio Berlusconi with the voters suggests that tricks and tricksters are still appreciated by Italians. Carnival has been revived in some cities, from Viareggio to Venice. When I was living in Venice in 1972, all I saw of Carnival was a few children wearing masks, but since 1979 it has become once again a public festival.

Other forms mix change with continuity. The tradition of Pasquino continues – indeed, the traditional site, Piazza Pasquino, is still in use for the purpose of protest – but the medium has changed, with the spraygun replacing the pen. The lottery survives, though it was nationalized in 1863, soon after the unification of Italy. One of the great Italian actors, the Neapolitan Antonio Clemente, known as Totò, fused the local tradition of stand-up comedians with that of the *commedia dell'arte*, thus creating a personal style that he adopted for both stage and screen.

The codification and standardization of play continued, though Italians no longer played a central role in the process. It was the British, for instance, who drew up the rules for whist in Edmond Hoyle's treatise (1742); for cricket (1744); for football (1863); and for boxing (the 'Queensberry Rules', 1867). The countrymen of Giovanni Maria de' Bardi, who codified Florentine football in the sixteenth century, adopted the new British system in the 1880s. The

---

[3] Paolo Toschi, *Le origini del teatro italiano* (Turin, 1955), 228ff., 308ff.

Epilogue: Beyond 1650

social separation of forms of play has continued. One sign of this separation has been the rise of a separate genre of children's books, including classics such as Carlo Collodi's *Pinocchio* (1883), which was turned into an Italian film in 1911 and a Walt Disney film in 1940.

Five Trends

Among the most important trends in the history of play since 1650 are the following five: proliferation, professionalization, commercialization, internationalization and civilization.

From the beginning of the nineteenth century, new leisure activities have proliferated and a whole new vocabulary has come into existence to describe these 'sports', 'hobbies' or 'entertainments', whether active – from bird-watching or stamp-collecting to computer games – or passive – reading novels, going to concerts or watching television. The media too have proliferated, with live performances joined by cheap print and then by film, radio, television, video and online entertainment. Works that originate in one medium are adapted to others. Andrea Camilleri's stories about Inspector Montalbano, published from 1994 onwards, have been a success both in print and in a television series that began to be shown in 1999. Given his interest in play, it is appropriate that Umberto Eco's literary *jeu d'esprit*, *The Name of the Rose* (1980), has been adapted a number of times into other media – film, a television series, board games and video games.

The balance between active and passive leisure has

gradually changed, so that we might speak of the slow but irresistible rise of the spectator as the complementary opposite of the professional performer for whom play is actually work, a career that leads for some to stardom. Performances have increasingly taken place in specialized locales: the theatre, the music hall, the cinema, the tennis court, the football pitch, the stadium or the race-track. In nineteenth-century Italy, for the bourgeoisie at least, Carnival had already become a time for going to performances of comic opera and melodrama, rather than for dressing as a harlequin or dancing in the street. Today, Carnival has become a spectacle to be watched on television, and it may even take place in a stadium such as the famous 'Sambadrome' of Rio de Janeiro.

Such performances illustrate the trend that the British historian J. H. Plumb described as 'the commercialization of leisure'.[4] Plumb argued that the trend began in the eighteenth century, when London, for instance, became the scene of concerts that were open to all who could pay for a ticket, as well as a major venue for boxing matches and circuses, while racing took place at Newmarket in Suffolk. Italy offers earlier examples of the trend. The Venetian opera-houses, for instance, opened in the seventeenth century.[5]

A major stimulus to commercialization was the rise of tourism, beginning with the foreign nobles who visited Italy on what became known as the 'Grand Tour', especially in the seventeenth and eighteenth centuries. In

---

[4] J. H. Plumb, *The Commercialization of Leisure in Eighteenth-Century England* (Reading, 1973).
[5] Simon Worsthorne, *Venetian Opera in the Seventeenth Century* (Oxford, 1954).

Epilogue: Beyond 1650

Venice, the traditional fist wars were sometimes staged out of season for the sake of important visitors.[6] Tourism itself is, of course, a form of play, allowing participants a brief escape from their everyday lives and identities. The age of mass tourism, especially from the 1950s onwards, when Italy became a major playground, has led to the increasing popularity – or even the revival – of a number of traditional games and festivals, whether they are staged to attract tourists or to support local patriotism. The reappearance of some traditional Italian festivals such as the Carnival of Venice has taken place for the sake of the tourists rather than for the declining population of the city. Today, tourists can also visit Pisa to watch the revived battle on the bridge, and Florence for the feast of San Giovanni, which now includes a re-enactment of the traditional form of *calcio* on Piazza San Croce. In Siena, the *palio* did not need to be revived, but it might now be said to have two different meanings: one for the Sienese, who know and care about which horse wins and cheer for their *contrada*; and the other for foreigners, who enjoy watching the procession before the race but are unable to discern which horse it was that won.

Mass tourism is one aspect of what might be called the internationalization of play in an age of both economic and cultural globalization, from the later nineteenth century onwards. Among its most visible forms are the many international championships, beginning with athletics. They depend on the standardization of the rules of the game, a major contrast with many forms of play

---

[6] Peter Burke, 'The Carnival of Venice', in *Historical Anthropology of Early Modern Italy* (Cambridge, 1987), 183–190, at 190.

Play in Renaissance Italy

in the Renaissance, which were organized locally and played according to local conventions.

The Olympic Games were founded – or, more exactly, re-founded – in 1896. In football, the World Cup was launched in 1930, and won by Italy in 1934, 1938, 1982 and 2006. Formula One goes back to 1946, while competition for the European Grand Prix began early in the twentieth century. Championships for players of chess, bridge and other games are too numerous to mention. They even include the traditional game of *morra*, following the foundation of the 'Italian Fingers Championship' in 2005.

International championships were and are supported by organizations such as FIFA (founded in 1903), the International Tennis Federation (1913) and the International Chess Federation (1924). Although regional teams – such as Lazio in Rome or Juventus in Turin – remain the object of fierce loyalties, the teams themselves became increasingly international in the later twentieth century. The Argentinian Diego Maradona played for Naples, while the Frenchman Zinedine Zidane played for Juventus. Football offers what are surely the most spectacular examples of both the globalization and the commercialization of play in the form of the enormous transfer fees paid by clubs in order to obtain star players. In 1992, for instance, Juventus paid what was then the record sum of about £15,000,000 for Gianluca Vialli, while in 2019 they paid about £67,000,000 for the Dutch player Matthijs de Ligt.

Another long-term trend, the taming of play – in other words, the gradual decline, or partial decline, of playful violence – is linked to what Norbert Elias, whose theory of sport was discussed in Chapter 1, famously called

Epilogue: Beyond 1650

the 'civilizing process': in other words, the rise of social pressures that encouraged or enforced a greater degree of self-control than before.[7] Readers of earlier chapters may well have been surprised at the violence of games in Renaissance Italy. Only towards the end of the period does this begin to change, as tournaments moved closer to ballet. In the seventeenth century, as was suggested in the previous chapter, the process went further. The Venetian stick wars became fist wars, while the annual race of Jews in Rome, who had been pelted with stones by the spectators, was abolished by the Pope in 1668. By the eighteenth century, the Venetian Carnival had become a civilized – or, if you prefer, a tame – affair where revellers played cards, went to the opera, or watched a female regatta – unlike its sixteenth-century predecessor, when death awaited a few participants.[8]

Moving forward to our own time, violence does, of course, survive in some sports, such as American football and British rugby, not to mention boxing. However, this violence is kept under control, something almost unthinkable in the Renaissance and certainly impossible to enforce at that time. Today, violent behaviour is more visible among the fans, in the stands or in the streets, than among the players.

All these trends are of interest to historians, and most of them have been studied, at least for certain places and periods. Syntheses are rarer. The material exists for books like this one about England in the age of Shakespeare, France in the age of Rabelais, Spain in

---

[7] Norbert Elias, *The Civilizing Process* (1939: English translation, Oxford, 1978); Elias and Eric Dunning, *Quest for Excitement: Sport and Leisure in the Civilizing Process* (Oxford, 1985).
[8] Davis, *The War of the Fists*, 53.

the age of Cervantes, or Germany in the age of the Reformation, a time when participants in the debate between Catholics and Protestants made use of what Mikhail Bakhtin called 'uncrowning' – in other words, the use of humour to destroy one's opponents. Other centuries and other parts of the world might also be approached from this angle. It is my hope that this attempt at an overview of one culture in one period will encourage more studies of this kind.

Dramatis Personae

Biographical notes on the principal players who have appeared in this essay.

Leonbattista Alberti (1404–72), a Florentine humanist and athlete as well as the author of mathematical games, the comedy *Momus*, and *Musca*, a praise of the fly.

Giangiorgio Alione (c. 1460–1529), from Asti, a nobleman, wrote ten farces in dialect.

Cristoforo 'Altissimo' (flourished c. 1500) was a singer of tales on Piazza San Martino in Florence.

Isabella Andreini (1562–1604), from Padua, an actress, joined the company of the *Gelosi* at the age of 14 and became famous in the role of their prima donna.

Giuseppe Arcimboldo (c. 1526–93), from Milan, was a painter in the service of three successive emperors in Vienna and Prague.

Pietro Aretino (1492–1556), from Arezzo, lived in Rome, Mantua and Venice, and wrote comedies, dialogues and satires.

Dramatis Personae

Lodovico Ariosto (1474–1533), a nobleman from Ferrara, wrote comedies as well as his famous poem *Orlando Furioso* (1516).

Adriano Banchieri (1568–1634), a monk from Bologna, wrote music and comedies in dialect.

Matteo Bandello (died *c.* 1560), a priest from Lombardy, wrote short stories (*novelle*).

Giovanni Maria de' Bardi (1534–1612), a Florentine patrician, wrote madrigals, plays and a treatise on *calcio*.

Girolamo Bargagli (1537–89), from Siena, a lawyer, wrote a play, *La Pellegrina*, and a dialogue on games.

Scipione Bargagli (1540–1612), younger brother of Girolamo, published *Imprese* (1578) and *Trattenimenti* (1587).

Carlo Maria Bascapè (1550–1615), from Milan, a disciple of Carlo Borromeo, became Bishop of Novara and, like Borromeo, a crusader against play.

Pietro Bembo (1470–1547), a Venetian humanist and cardinal. His book of jests was not published until the nineteenth century.

Angelo Beolco, nicknamed 'Ruzzante' (*c.* 1496–1542), was an actor and playwright from the countryside near Padua.

Bernardino da Siena (1380–1444) was a Franciscan friar and a critic of play in his popular sermons.

Francesco Berni (*c.* 1497–1535) was a comic poet active in Florence and in Rome, and an enemy of Aretino.

Jacopo Bonfadio (*c.* 1508–50), from Garda, was a humanist poet, philosopher and historian who wrote a burlesque about the gods.

Carlo Borromeo (1538–84), Archbishop of Milan and

Dramatis Personae

a cardinal, was the leader of a crusade against many forms of play.

Poggio Bracciolini (1380–1459) was a Tuscan humanist and author of a jestbook published in 1470.

Giovanni Briccio (1579–1645), from Rome, was a painter, playwright and singer.

Angelo Bronzino (1503–72), from Florence, was a painter and a comic poet.

Michelangelo Buonarroti (1475–1564) came from Florence. Besides his contribution to sculpture, painting and architecture, he produced comic sketches and poems.

Michelangelo Buonarroti the younger (1568–1646), great-nephew of the artist, was a Florentine courtier and playwright.

'Burchiello' (Domenico di Giovanni, 1404–49), from Florence, was famous for his nonsense verse.

Andrea Calmo (1510–71), a Venetian actor and playwright, is known for his comic letters.

Pietro Antonio Caracciolo (c. 1460 – c. 1531), from Naples, was an actor who also wrote farces in dialect.

Alessandro Caravia (1503–68), from Venice, was a goldsmith, and a comic poet in Venetian dialect.

Girolamo Cardano (1501–76), from Pavia, was a mathematician, astrologer, physician, gambler and author of a treatise on games of chance.

Annibale Caro (1507–66), a writer from the Marche and a secretary to the Farnese family, was the author of a comedy and some parodies.

Ludovico Castelvetro (1505–71), a humanist from Modena, discussed humour in his commentary on Aristotle's *Poetics*.

Dramatis Personae

'Cherea' (Francesco de' Nobili, flourished 1508–32) came from Lucca and was an actor in Venice and Rome.

Giulio Cesare Croce (1550–1609), from Bologna, was an artisan, a dialect poet and the creator of the character Bertoldo.

Giovanni Della Casa (1503–56) was a Florentine archbishop best known for his conduct book *Il Galateo*, which criticized some forms of play, though he had been a 'playboy' himself in his youth.

Lodovico Dolce (1508–68) was a professional writer active in Venice whose work includes comedies and comic poems.

Lodovico Domenichi (1515–64), from Piacenza, was a professional writer active in Venice, the author of comedies and editor of a jestbook.

Giovanni Dominici (1356–1419), from Florence, was a Dominican friar who became a cardinal and criticized many forms of play.

Antonfrancesco Doni (1513–74), from Florence, became a professional writer in Venice and wrote comic dialogues and a commentary on the verses of Burchiello.

Bernardo Dovizi ('Bibbiena', 1470–1520), a diplomat, wrote a comedy and appears as a jester in Castiglione's *Book of the Courtier*.

Alfonso II d'Este, (1533–97), Duke of Ferrara, was an enthusiast for games, especially ball games.

Agnolo Firenzuola (1493–1553) was a Florentine monk who became a secular priest and wrote comedies and comic poems.

Teofilo Folengo (1491–1544), a noble from the region of Mantua, became a Benedictine monk and later a mac-

Dramatis Personae

aronic poet, writing under the pseudonym Merlinus Coccaius.

Fabrizio de Fornaris (c. 1550 – c. 1585) was a Neapolitan actor famous in the role of Capitano Coccodrillo, and also the author of a comedy, *Angelica*.

Niccolò Franco (1515–70), from Benevento, Aretino's secretary, wrote sonnets against his employer and was hanged for writing against Pope Paul IV.

Gian Maria Giberti (1495–1543) was a leading cleric in Rome and patron of Berni and Mauro, before becoming the reforming Bishop of Verona.

Pietro Gonnella (c. 1390–1441), a buffoon at the court of Ferrara. His portrait was painted by Jean Fouquet.

Antonfrancesco Grazzini (1505–84), known as 'Lasca', was a Florentine pharmacist who wrote comic poems and edited those of his contemporaries.

Giovanni Battista Lalli (1572–1637), from Norcia, was the author of mock-epics.

Ortensio Lando (1510 – c. 1558), from Milan, became a friar and then a professional writer in Venice and elsewhere, best known for his paradoxes and parodies.

Roland de Lassus (1532–94), also known as Orlando Lasso, was a musician from the Netherlands who acted and played the fool at the court of Munich.

Roberto da Lecce (c. 1425–95) was a Franciscan friar and a critic of dancing.

Zuan Polo Liompardi (died 1541) was a Venetian comic actor.

Gian Paolo Lomazzo (1538–92), a painter from Milan, was also a writer on art theory and the head of a festive society, the *Accademia della Valle di Blegno*.

Vincenzo Maggi (1498–1564), from Brescia, studied and

Dramatis Personae

taught at Padua before moving to Ferrara as a tutor to Prince Alfonso. He published a treatise on humour.

Arlotto Mainardi, Il Piovano (1396–1484) was a Florentine priest and jester. His collection of comic anecdotes was published posthumously.

Francesco Marcolini (d. 1559), a bookseller from Forlì, moved to Venice and published works by Aretino and Doni, as well as his own parlour game, the *Sorti*.

Giovanni Mauro (c. 1489–1535), a nobleman from Friuli, lived in Rome as secretary to a cardinal and wrote his comic verses there.

Francesco Maria Molza (1489–1544) was a poet from Modena who lived in Rome, and is best known for his mock-eulogies.

Pier Francesco Orsini (1523–85), known as 'Vicino', a member of a powerful noble family, was the owner (and perhaps the designer) of the garden of Bomarzo.

Francesco Petrarca ('Petrarch') (1304–74), a Tuscan poet and humanist, was also the author of a book of jests.

Agnolo Poliziano (1454–94) was a Tuscan humanist and also author of a jestbook.

Giovanni Pontano (1426–1503), a humanist from Umbria active in Naples, wrote about humour in his treatise on speech, *De sermone*.

Giambattista della Porta (c. 1535–1615), who lived in Naples, was a polymath whose works included comedies.

Luigi Pulci (1432–84), a poet and diplomat in the household of Lorenzo de' Medici, was the author of the mock-epic *Morgante*.

Innocentio Ringhieri (c. 1500 – c. 1580), from Bologna, was the author of a treatise on games.

Dramatis Personae

Annibale Romei (flourished c. 1565 – c. 1585), a courtier and chess player in Ferrara, included a description of different games in his *Discourses* (1585).

Francesco Sansovino (1521–86) was active in Venice as a bookseller and a professional writer whose work included comic poems.

Girolamo Savonarola (1452–98), from Ferrara, was a Dominican friar and a crusader against many forms of play, especially in Florence.

Antonio Scaino (1524–1612), from Salò, was a nobleman, a priest and a diplomat in Ferrara, who wrote a book on tennis for Duke Alfonso.

Domenigo Taiacalze (died 1513) was a Venetian comic actor.

Torquato Tasso (1544–95) was a courtier in Ferrara who wrote discourses on games as well as his famous poems.

Alessandro Tassoni (1565–1635) was a patrician from Modena and the author of a mock-epic about the theft of a bucket.

Claudio Tolomei (1492–1556), from a leading family of Siena, was a diplomat, poet and critic who became Bishop of Korcula.

Arcangelo Tuccaro (1535–1602) was an Italian acrobat who also published a book about his art.

Benedetto Varchi (1503–65) was a Florentine humanist whose comic works include a comedy and songs for Carnival.

Orazio Vecchi (1550–1605) was a musician from Modena who wrote plays composed of madrigals.

Lorenzo Venier (1510–50) was a Venetian patrician, a disciple of Aretino and the author of *Il Trentuno della Zaffetta* and *La Puttana Errante*.

Dramatis Personae

Maffio Venier (1550–86), a Venetian patrician, was the author of satire and pornographic poetry in Venetian dialect.

Nicola Villani (1590–1636), from Pistoia, was a poet and the author of a history of comic poetry.

Further Reading

A selection of important studies in English.

Richard Andrews (1993) *Scripts and Scenarios: The Performance of Comedy in Renaissance Italy*, Cambridge

Sydney Anglo (2000) *The Martial Arts of Renaissance Europe*, New Haven, CT

Alessandro Arcangeli (1994) 'Dance Under Trial: The Moral Debate, 1200–1600', *Dance Research* 12, 127–55

Alessandro Arcangeli (2003) *Recreation in the Renaissance: Attitudes Towards Leisure and Pastimes in European Culture, 1350–1700*, Basingstoke

Mikhail Bakhtin (1929) *Problems of Dostoyevsky's Poetics*, English translation, Manchester, 1984

Mikhail Bakhtin (1965) *Rabelais and his World*, English translation, Cambridge, MA, 1968

Paul Barolsky (1978) *Infinite Jest: Wit and Humor in Italian Renaissance Art*, Columbia, MO

Further Reading

Cees de Bondt (2006) *Royal Tennis in Renaissance Italy*, Turnhout

Peter Burke (1978) *Popular Culture in Early Modern Europe*, 3rd edn, Farnham, 2009

Roger Caillois (1958) *Man, Play and Games*, English translation, London, 1962

Linda L. Carroll (1990) *Angelo Beolco (il Ruzante)*, Boston, MA

Thomas F. Crane (1920) 'Parlor Games', in *Italian Social Customs of the Sixteenth Century*, New Haven, CT, 263–322

Robert C. Davis (1994) *The War of the Fists: Popular Culture and Public Violence in Late Renaissance Venice*, New York

Charles Dempsey (2001) *Inventing the Renaissance Putto*, Chapel Hill, NC

Michael Dummett (2004) *A History of Games Played with the Tarot Pack*, Oxford

Alan Dundes and Alessandro Falassi (1975) *La Terra in Piazza: An Interpretation of the Palio of Siena*, Berkeley, CA

Clifford Geertz (1973) 'Deep Play', in *The Interpretation of Cultures*, New York, 412–53

Ernst H. Gombrich (1986) 'Architecture and Rhetoric in Giulio Romano's Palazzo del Te', in *New Light on Old Masters*, Oxford, 161–70

Ernst Gombrich and Ernst Kris (1940) *Caricature*, London

Robert Henke (1997) 'The Italian Mountebank and the *Commedia dell'Arte*', *Theatre Survey* 39, 1–29

Robert Henke (2002) *Performance and Literature in the Commedia dell'Arte*, Cambridge

Further Reading

Marvin T. Herrick (1960) *Italian Comedy in the Renaissance*, Urbana, IL

Johan Huizinga (1938) *Homo Ludens: A Study of the Play Element in Culture*, English translation, 2nd edn, London, 1970

Thomas DaCosta Kaufmann (2010) *Arcimboldo: Visual Jokes, Natural History and Still-Life Painting*, Chicago, IL

Claudia Lazzaro (1990) *The Italian Renaissance Garden*, New Haven, CT

Kathleen Lea (1934) *Italian Popular Comedy*, Oxford

Rebekka von Mallinkrodt and Angela Schattner (eds., 2016) *Sports and Physical Exercise in Early Modern Culture*, Abingdon

Giuseppe Mazzotta (1986) *The World at Play in Boccaccio's Decameron*, Princeton, NJ

John McClelland (2013–14) 'Sport and Scientific Thinking in the Sixteenth Century: Ruling Out Playfulness', *Ludica* 19–20, 134–45

George McClure (2008) 'Women and the Politics of Play in Sixteenth-Century Italy', *Renaissance Quarterly* 61, 750–91

George McClure (2013) *Parlour Games and the Public Life of Women in Renaissance Italy*, Toronto

Luke Morgan (2016) *The Monster in the Garden*, Philadelphia, PA

Franco Mormando (1999) *The Preacher's Demons: Bernardino of Siena and the Social Underground of Early Renaissance Italy*, Chicago, IL

H. J. R. Murray (1913) *A History of Chess*, Oxford

Anthony Newcomb (1980) *The Madrigal at Ferrara*, Princeton, NJ

Further Reading

Oystein Ore (1953) *Cardano, the Gambling Scholar*, Princeton, NJ

Gherardo Ortalli (1995) 'Uncertain Thresholds of Tolerance: Games and Crisis in the Middle Ages', *Ludica* 1, 56–68

Gherardo Ortalli (2013–14) 'Sixteenth-Century Courts and Salons: *giochi di veglia*', *Ludica* 19–20, 61–86

Gherardo Ortalli (ed., 2019) *Lotteries, Lotto, Slot Machines. The Luck of the Draw: A History of Games of Chance*, Treviso

Kenneth Richards and Laura Richards (eds., 1991) *The Commedia dell'arte: A Documentary History*, Oxford

Robert J. Rodini (1970) *A. F. Grazzini*, Madison, WI

Margaret F. Rosenthal (1992) *The Honest Courtesan: Veronica Franco*, Chicago, IL

Jessie Sheeler (2007) *The Garden at Bomarzo: A Renaissance Riddle*, London

Simone Testa (2015) *Italian Academies and Their Networks, 1525–1700*, Basingstoke

Richard C. Trexler (1981) *Public Life in Renaissance Florence*, New York

Jonathan Walker (1999) 'Gambling and Venetian Noblemen, c. 1500–1700', *Past and Present* 162, 28–69

Elissa Weaver (2002) *Convent Theatre in Early Modern Italy*, Cambridge

Domenico Zanrè (2004) *Cultural Nonconformity in Early Modern Florence*, Aldershot

Index

academies, 103–5
  Crusca, 104
  Florentine, 103
  Humidi, 105
  Intronati, 103–5, 107
  Lincei, 104
  Platonic, 103
  Valle di Bregno, 46, 105
  Vignaioli, 103, 105
acrobatics, 27–8, 59
Ademollo, Alessandro, 15
Alberti, Leon Battista, 4, 23, 36,
  38, 49, 75, 79–80, 94
Alione, Giangiorgio, 56
Andreini, Isabella, 60, 96
Andrelini, Fausto, 78–9
Antoniano, Silvio, 81
Arcimboldo, Giuseppe, 3, 52
Aretino, Pietro, 14, 33, 38, 45,
  49–50, 57, 63, 71, 82, 93,
  127–8
Ariès, Philippe, 15
Ariosto, Ludovico, 4, 35, 42,
  46, 49–50, 57, 91, 106,
  111, 128
Aristotle, 41, 83
Armani, Vincenza, 96
Arnigio, Bartolomeo, 137

art, play in, 51–4
Atanagi, Dionisio, 91
athletics, 23, 81, 143–4

backgammon, 34
Baglione, Giovanni, 44, 65
Bakhtin, Mikhail Mikhailovich,
  6, 15–16, 43, 66, 113, 135,
  146
Banchieri, Adriano, 30, 94, 131
Bandello, Matteo, 62, 69, 94,
  102, 128
Barberini, Antonio, 130–1
Barbino, Pietro, 88–9
Bardi, Alessandro de', 135
Bardi, Giovanni Maria de', 140
Bargagli, Girolamo, 12, 21,
  34, 36, 49, 81, 83, 92, 99,
  102–3, 107, 109, 127, 136
Bargagli, Scipione, 36, 99
Baroja, Júlio Caro, 15
Barolsky, Paul, 51
Bascapè, Carlo Maria, 83,
  124–6
Battiferri, Laura, 96
Battistin, 87
bear-baiting, 28
beffa, 9, 18, 60–6, 69, 132

159

Index

Belcari, Feo, 129
Bellarmino, Roberto, 124–5, 127
Bellini, Giovanni, 51
Bembo, Pietro, 3, 43, 94
Benetton Foundation, 18
Benivieni, Girolamo, 78
Bentivoglio, Diana Saliceto, 97
Bentivoglio, Margherita, 99
Beolco, Angelo, *see* 'Ruzzante'
Berlusconi, Silvio, 140
Bernardino da Siena, 77–8, 123
Berni, Francesco, 3, 9, 38, 43, 48–9, 71, 83, 103, 128
Bernini, Gianlorenzo, 131
Bibbiena, Bernardo da, 40, 43, 57, 82, 92, 119
board games, 34, *see also* chess
Boccaccio, Giovanni, vii, 10, 31, 35, 61–2, 83, 98, 102
Bocchi, Achille, 105
Boiteux, Martine, 19
Bologna, 42, 46, 51, 62, 65, 94, 105, 115, 118, 120, 130
Bomarzo, 7, 53–4, 83, 110–13
Bonfadio, Jacopo, 49
boredom, 9
Borgia, Cesare, 28, 69
    Lucrezia, 57
Borromeo, Carlo, 124–8
Bourdieu, Pierre, 106
Braccio di Bartolo, 'Morgante', 88
Bracciolini, Poggio, 3, 43
Bredekamp, Horst, 19
Briccio, Giovanni, 131
Bronzino, Angelo, 3, 83, 88
Browning, Robert, 67
Brunelleschi, Filippo, 37, 61, 63–4
Bruno, Giordano, 2, 4, 41, 85
buffoons, 10, 42, 78, 88
bulls, 27–8, 107–8, 116–17, 125

Buonarotti, Michelangelo, 3, 51, 92
Buonarotti, Michelangelo, the younger, 131
Buontalenti, Bernardo, 54
Burchiello, Domenico, 44–5, 91, 128
Burckhardt, Jacob, 13, 37, 63, 66–8, 72, 109, 113

Caillois, Roger, 5, 36, 121
Cajetan, Tommaso, 79
Calmo, Andrea, 10, 59, 90, 128
Camilleri, Andrea, 141
Cantastorie, cantimbanchi, 90, 108
Caprarola, 54
Caracciolo, Pietro Antonio, 2, 56
Caracciolo, Roberto, *see* Roberto da Lecce
Caravaggio (Michelangelo Merisi), 44, 65
Caravia, Alessandro, 10, 26, 48, 68
Cardano, Girolamo, 12, 33, 82, 84
cards, 32–3, 84
caricature, 132–3
Carnival, 6–7, 69–70, 113, 116–22, 125–7, 129–31, 135, 140, 142, 145
Caro, Annibale, 13, 38, 50, 103, 111
Caro Baroja, Julio, 15
Caroto, Giovanni Francesco, 101
Carracci family, 51, 132
Castelvetro, Lodovico, 38, 41
Castiglione, Baldassare, 3, 9, 24, 31, 40–1, 43, 50, 82, 93–4, 98, 128, 135–6
Celle, Giovanni dalle, 82
charlatans, 55, 91, 108
Cherea, 87

160

Index

chess, 34, 81, 99, 144
children, 100–1, 134, 141
Christine of Lorraine, 24
Cicero, 41
Citolini, Alessandro, 100
clowns, *see* buffoons
cock-fights, 16–17, 28
codification, 133–4, 140
Collodi, Carlo, 141
Colonna, Vittoria, 96
commedia dell'arte, 45–7, 56, 59, 68–9
commercialization, 142–3
competition, 36–9
Coppa, Jacopo, 90
Corsaro, Antonio, 19
Crane, Thomas F., 14
Cristoforo 'Altissimo', 90
Croce, Benedetto, 14
Croce, Giulio Cesare, 42, 46, 49, 60, 89–90, 130
Culianu, Ioan Petru, 17

dance, 28–9, 59, 76–9, 96, 135
Dante, 46, 111–12
deceit, 9, 11, 42, 60, 62, 64, 69, 71, 90, 140, *see also* beffa
deep play, 32
deformity, 40, 54
Della Casa, Giovanni, 38, 40, 43–4, 71, 82, 94, 103, 124, 136
Della Porta, Giambattista, 2
Democritus, 85
dialect, 45–6, 56–7, 59–60
dice, 32–3, 35, 72, 84–5
Dolce, Lodovico, 91
Domenichi, Lodovico, 43, 91, 111, 128
Dominici, Giovanni, 77–8, 101
Donatello (Donato Bardi), 52, 64
Doni, Antonfrancesco, 38, 91
draughts, 34
Ducci, Agostino di, 52

Dundes, Alan, 26
Dunning, Eric, 17
dwarves, 40, 88–9, 109

Eco, Umberto, 86, 141
Elias, Norbert, 17, 20, 144–5
enigmas, 36, 111
Este
  Alfonso d', 22
  Beatrice, 64, 96, 97, 106
  Isabella, 4, 88, 96, 106
  Leonora, 99

farces, 56
Federico of Urbino, Duke, 68
Ferrara, 21–2, 88, 96, 106, 130
Ficino, Marsilio, 4, 80, 85
Firenzuola, Agnolo, 94
Folengo, Teofilo, 45, 47–8, 62, 94
Fonti, Sigismondo, 33, 35
fools, *see* buffoons
football, 24–5, 140–1, 144
Fornaris, Fabrizio de, 2
Fortini, Pietro, 137
fortune telling, 33, 35, 114, 126–7, 137
Fracastoro, Girolamo, 77
Franco, Niccolò, 71
Franco, Veronica, 70
Frazer, James, 15
Freud, Sigmund, 16, 44

Galilei, Galileo, 4, 41
Gambara, Veronica, 96
gambling, 36–7, 76–7, 84, 136
games of chance, 32–3, 82
gardens, 53–4, 88, 109–13
Garzoni, Tommaso, 128
Geertz, Clifford, 16–17, 32
Gelli, Giambattista, 101
Ghiberti, Lorenzo, 37
giants, 53, 109, 111, 116
Giberti, Gian Maria, 78
Giorgione, 92

161

Index

Giraldi Cinthio, Giambattista, 55
Giulio Romano, 3, 53
Goldoni, Carlo, 56
Gonnella, Pietro, 13, 88
Gonzaga, Elisabetta, 96, 98
Graf, Arturo, 14
Grazzini, Antonfrancesco, 'il Lasca', 48, 62, 69, 93, 97
Greeks, 47
Gregory XIII, Pope, 125
Gualtieri, Lorenzo, 35
Guarini, Battista, 106–7
Guasti, Cesare, 14
guessing games, 35

Harff, Anton von, 117
Hatton, Christopher, 28
Henke, Robert, 55–6
Heywood, William, 15
holidays, 139
horsemanship, 23, 96–7, 108, 131, 134
Hoyle, Edmond, 140
Huizinga, Johan, 5, 7, 37, 42, 68
humanism, 88
hunting, 23, 28, 81, 96–7, 108

Imprese, 36, 81
insults, 70
Israeli, Isaac D', 13–14

Josquin des Prez, 30
jousts, 23–4
Juventus, 144

Lalli, Giovanni Battista, 133
Lando, Ortensio, 91, 94
Lassus, Roland de, 30
Lazio, 144
leisure, 139–42
Leo X, Pope, 3, 88, 102
Leonardo, 3, 10, 92
Ligt, Matthijs de, 144

Liompardi, Zuan Polo, 59, 87, 90
Lomazzo, Gianpaolo, 46–7
Longhi, Silvia, 19
Loredan, Gianfrancesco, 133
Lucrezia da Siena, 96

macaronic verse, 45
Machiavelli, Niccolò, 4, 23, 34, 60–1, 69, 92
madrigals, 30, 83
Maggi, Vincenzo, 41
Mainardi, Arlotto, 13, 43, 94, 128–9
Mantua, 88, 106
Maradona, Diego, 144
Marcolini, Francesco, 34–5
Mariano, Fra (Mariano Fetti), 88
Masuccio Salernitano, 62
Mauro, Giovanni, 49
Medici,
  Catherine de', 99
  Cosimo de', 3
  Grand Duke Cosimo I de', 83–4, 88
  Grand Duke Ferdinando de', 24, 107
  Grand Duke Francesco de', 54
  Giovanni de' (Leo X), 3, 88, 102
  Giuliano de', 24
  Isabella de', 99
  Lorenzo de', 3, 24, 48, 92, 112
Mercuriale, Girolamo, 12, 23, 80
Michelangelo, 3, 51, 92
Milan, 46, 64, 94, 128–9, 139
mock battles, 23–5, 28, 76–7, 95
mock commentaries, 50
mock-epics, 46–8, 133
mock epitaphs, 49

Index

mock eulogies, 49
mock sieges, 28
Molino, Antonio, 45
Molza, Francesco Maria, 50, 103
Montaigne, Michel de, 54
Montefeltro, Federico da, *see* Federico of Urbino
Monteverdi, Claudio, 107
Muratori, Ludovico, 12–13
music, 29–30, 78, 92, 95–6, 107
Musset, Alfred de, 67

Naples, 2, 29, 67, 95, 140, 144
Neri, Filippo, 129
Nicholas of Cusa, 85

Orlando Lasso, 30
Ortalli, Gherardo, 19
Orsini, Vicino, 53, 110–13

pageants, 114, 117
Paleotti, Gabriele, 124–5, 128
palio, 26–7, 143, *see also* races
Parabosco, Girolamo, 132
'parlour games', 14, 33–4, 98
parody, 46–7, 51
Pasquino, 57–8, 140
Passarotti, Bartolomeo, 51
Paul II, Pope, 27
Paul III, Pope, 136
Pazzi, Alfonso de', 38
Perugia, 26, 77–8, 104
Petrarch, 3, 35, 43, 46, 49, 56, 75
Peverara, Laura, 96
Pia, Emilia, 98
Piero della Francesca, 68
Pisa, 26, 143
Pitrè, Giuseppe, 15, 139
Pius IV, Pope, 124–5
Plato, 80, 85, 103
Plautus, 56–7, 59–60, 106
plays, 55–60, 96, 102, 105–7, 114, 119, 125–6, 129, 131, 135, *see also commedia dell'arte*
Plumb, J. H., 142
Poggio, *see* Bracciolini
Poliziano, Angelo, 3, 24, 43
Pomponazzi, Pietro, 75
Pontano, Giovanni, 41–2, 82
Pratolino, 54
printing, 22, 34, 91–2, 134
Procaccioli, Paolo, 19
Pulci, Luigi, 24, 48, 88, 111
puppets, 2, 69
putti, 52–3

Rabelais, François, 16, 62, 66, 94, 111
races, 26–7, 131, 144
Raphael, 3, 52, 92
Ray, John, 131
riding, *see* horsemanship
Ringhieri, Innocenzo, 34, 81, 99, 102
Rizzi, Alessandra, 19
Roberto da Lecce, 77, 100
Romei, Annibale, 35
Rosa, Salvatore, 131
Ruzzante (Angelo Beolco), 57, 90

Sabadino degli Arienti, Giovanni, 62, 72
Sacchetti, Francesco, 62
Salernitano, Masuccio, 1, 62
Sanseverino, Barbara, 97
Sansovino, Francesco, 91, 111, 153
Sanudo, Marin, 76, 97, 117
Savonarola, Girolamo, 77–8, 123
Scafoglio, Domenico, 19
Scaino, Antonio, 22, 81, 94, 97
self-control, 17, 93, 145
Seneca the Younger, 55
serious play, 4, 85–6, 105, 134

Index

Sforza, Ludovico, Duke of Milan, 64
Shakespeare, William, 57, 60, 96
shame, 71
Sicily, 2, 131–2, 139
Siena, 26–7, 38, 68, 109, 143
Sixtus V, Pope, 125
Speroni, Sperone, 75
Spirto, Lorenzo, 33, 127
sport, 17, 133
Stampa, Gaspara, 96
Strozzi, Marietta degli, 95
surprise, 53
Symonds, John Addington, 13

Taiacalze, Domenico, 59, 90
Tasso, Torquato, 46, 83, 99, 106
Tassoni, Alessandro, 47, 133
tennis, 25, 144
Tesauro, Emmanuele, 132
Thompson, Stith, 61
Tibaldi, Pellegrino, 51
Tintoretto (Jacopo Robusti), 51
Tiraboschi, Girolamo, 12–13
Titian (Tiziano Vecelli), 51
Tolomei, Claudio, 94
Toscan, Jean, 44
Totò (Antonio Clemente), 140
tournaments, 23–4, 75, 81, 97, 130, 145

tourism, 142–3
tricks, tricksters, *see* deceit
Trissino, Giangiorgio, 55
Tubaldino, Simone, 129
Tullia d'Aragona, 96
Turcaro, Arcangelo, 80

uncrowning, 6, 16, 70, 146

Varchi, Benedetto, 38, 92, 104
Vasari, Giorgio, 10, 54
Veblen, Thorstein, 93
Vecchi, Orazio, 30, 83
Venier, Lorenzo, 69–70
Venier, Maffio, 71
Vettori, Piero, 82
Vialli, Gianluca, 144
Vida, Girolamo, 34
Villamont, Seigneur de, 119
Villani, Nicola, 12
violence, 66–73, 107, 120, 127, 130, 145
visual play, 51–4
Vittorino da Feltre, 80–1

Warburg, Aby, 15
withdrawal of upper classes, 29, 79, 134–5

Zaffetta, Anzola, 69–70
Zidane, Zinedine, 144
Zuan Polo (Liompardi), 87, 90

Dramatis Personae

Biographical notes on the principal players who have appeared in this essay.

Leonbattista Alberti (1404–72), a Florentine humanist and athlete as well as the author of mathematical games, the comedy *Momus*, and *Musca*, a praise of the fly.

Giangiorgio Alione (c. 1460–1529), from Asti, a nobleman, wrote ten farces in dialect.

Cristoforo 'Altissimo' (flourished c. 1500) was a singer of tales on Piazza San Martino in Florence.

Isabella Andreini (1562–1604), from Padua, an actress, joined the company of the *Gelosi* at the age of 14 and became famous in the role of their prima donna.

Giuseppe Arcimboldo (c. 1526–93), from Milan, was a painter in the service of three successive emperors in Vienna and Prague.

Pietro Aretino (1492–1556), from Arezzo, lived in Rome, Mantua and Venice, and wrote comedies, dialogues and satires.

Dramatis Personae

Lodovico Ariosto (1474–1533), a nobleman from Ferrara, wrote comedies as well as his famous poem *Orlando Furioso* (1516).

Adriano Banchieri (1568–1634), a monk from Bologna, wrote music and comedies in dialect.

Matteo Bandello (died *c.* 1560), a priest from Lombardy, wrote short stories (*novelle*).

Giovanni Maria de' Bardi (1534–1612), a Florentine patrician, wrote madrigals, plays and a treatise on *calcio*.

Girolamo Bargagli (1537–89), from Siena, a lawyer, wrote a play, *La Pellegrina*, and a dialogue on games.

Scipione Bargagli (1540–1612), younger brother of Girolamo, published *Imprese* (1578) and *Trattenimenti* (1587).

Carlo Maria Bascapè (1550–1615), from Milan, a disciple of Carlo Borromeo, became Bishop of Novara and, like Borromeo, a crusader against play.

Pietro Bembo (1470–1547), a Venetian humanist and cardinal. His book of jests was not published until the nineteenth century.

Angelo Beolco, nicknamed 'Ruzzante' (*c.* 1496–1542), was an actor and playwright from the countryside near Padua.

Bernardino da Siena (1380–1444) was a Franciscan friar and a critic of play in his popular sermons.

Francesco Berni (*c.* 1497–1535) was a comic poet active in Florence and in Rome, and an enemy of Aretino.

Jacopo Bonfadio (*c.* 1508–50), from Garda, was a humanist poet, philosopher and historian who wrote a burlesque about the gods.

Carlo Borromeo (1538–84), Archbishop of Milan and